FASTSTART

YOUR

CORPORATION

The Essentials for Starting
Your Small Business Corporation

Ronika Khanna CPA, CA, CFA

Disclaimer

The author of this book and the accompanying materials has used their best efforts in preparing this book. The author makes no representation or warranties with respect to the accuracy, applicability, fitness, or completeness of the contents of this book. The information contained in this book is strictly for educational purposes. Therefore, if you wish to apply ideas contained in this book, you are taking full responsibility for your actions.

Contents

To the Reader 5

Introduction...7

Navigation 9

Part 1: Incorporation 11

Best Practices for New Corporations...13

What Are the Different Types of Business Structures in Canada? .17
  Business Structures 17

Why You Should Incorporate Your Small Business.......................19
  Which Structure Is Best? 19
  Other Factors to Consider 21

Corporations with One Client: Employee vs Self Employed 25
  Criteria to Determine Self Employment..................................... 25
  What Are the Implications of Being a Self-Employed Owner vs an
  Employee?... 26

How to Start Your Corporation 29
  Where to Incorporate: Federal or Provincial 29
  How to Choose a Corporate Name 31
  How to Set-Up Your Corporate Structure 40
  How to Get Incorporated 44

The Corporate Year End and How to Choose One 49
  How to Select a Year End for a Corporation.............................. 49
  What Are the Implications of Your Year End?............................. 51

Corporate Maintenance 53
  Annual Meetings 53
  Annual Return 54

From Sole Proprietorship to Corporation 55
  Steps to Take When Transitioning from a Sole Proprietorship to a
  Corporation 55

Part 2: Accounting **59**

Setting Up a Separate Bank and Credit Card Account 61
Why You Need to Have a Separate Corporate Bank Account 61
What Do You Need to Set Up a Business Bank Account? 63
Why You Should Also Have a Separate Credit Card for Your Business .. 64
Other Factors to Consider When Opening a Bank Account 65

What Type of Accounting Reports Do You Need for a Corporation?
....67
Financial Statements 67

Accounting Terms that Every Business Owner Should Know 71

Should You Do Your Own Small Business Accounting?.................**81**

What Are Your Options for Doing Your Accounting?....................**85**
Use a Spreadsheet... 85
Use Accounting Software 85
Outsource to an Accountant 91

How to Invoice Your Customers/Clients......................................**93**
How to Prepare an Invoice... 93
Information to Put on an Invoice: 94
Sales Tax and Invoicing.. 94

What to Look For in an Accountant? **97**

Part 3: Tax... **99**

What Are the Obligations for a Typical Corporation?.................**101**
Sales Tax Returns 101
Payroll Filings: 101
Dividend Declarations 102
Corporate Income Tax Returns 102
Annual Returns.. 102

What Is Sales Tax and Should You Register?..............................**105**
Should You Register Even If You Expect Less than $30,000 in Annual
Sales?... 106
What Does It Mean to Be Zero-Rated? 108
What Are Exempt Supplies and How Are They Different from Zero-
Rated? 109

Should You Opt for the Quick Method of Reporting GST/HST? ..111

What Are the Eligibility Criteria to Use the Quick Method? 111

What Are the Rates Used for the Quick Method? 112

When to Use the Quick Method 112

How to Register for the Quick Method 113

What You Need to Know about Registering for Sales Tax 115

How to Register for GST/HST 115

What Type of Information Do You Need to Register? 116

What Happens after You Register? 117

How to Pay GST/HST Using Online Banking 118

What Are the GST/HST Rates in each Province? 120

What Are the Penalties for Late Filing Your GST/HST Returns? 120

How to Pay Yourself from a Corporation: Salary vs Dividend 123

Do You Plan to Pay Yourself a Salary or Hire Employees? 127

How to Register for a Federal Payroll Account 129

What are Your Options for Preparing Your Payroll? 130

How Do You Pay Monthly Remittances (Deductions at Source) to
Revenue Canada? 132

What Are Your Year End Payroll Obligations? 134

How to Pay Yourself Dividends 135

Can You Borrow Money from the Corporation? 137

Shareholder Loan Balances 137

Exceptions for Shareholder Loans for Specific Purposes 138

Accounting for Shareholder Loans 139

What You Should Know about Corporate Tax...........................141

What Types of Expenses Are Deductible?...................................145

Types of Deductible Business Expenses 145

Other Considerations for Business Expenses 146

Pre-Incorporation Expenses 147

How to Sign Up for *My Business Account* with CRA 151

Benefits of Registering for *My Business Account* with CRA.................. 151

How to Register for *My Business Account*.................................... 153

What Are the Tax Filing Deadlines for a Corporation? 155

Corporate Income Tax Returns 155

Annual Returns 155

Sales Tax Filings 155

Payroll Filings 156

Dividend Declarations 156

Instalments 157

Investment Strategies for Incorporated Business Owners 159

Large Banking Institutions 160

Online Banks 160

Robo Advisors 161

Real Estate 161

Appendices 163

Appendix A: What You Need to Know about Having a Corporation in Quebec 165

Corporate Names in Quebec 165

How to Register Your Partnership or Corporation 166

Registering for RQ *My Account for Business*: clicSÉQUR 167

How to Register for 168

How to Register for Sales Tax in Quebec 169

What Are the Eligibility Criteria to Use the Quick Method in Quebec? 171

How Do You Register for a Quebec Payroll Account? 171

What You Need to Know about Corporate Taxes in Quebec 174

Appendix B: Sales Tax in Other Provinces 177

British Columbia Provincial Sales Tax (PST) 178

Manitoba Provincial Retail Sales Tax (RST) 180

Saskatchewan Provincial Sales Tax (PST) 181

About the Author 183

Other Books by Ronika Khanna 185

TO THE READER

Complimentary PDF Version with Links

Throughout this book there are links to various resources that do not appear in the print version. If you would like a complimentary version of the PDF with links, please email me at ronika@montrealfinancial.ca along with proof of purchase, and I would be happy to send it to you.

Reviews and Feedback

If you find this book useful, I would greatly appreciate a testimonial or review on the website where you purchased it.

Alternatively, if you think the book doesn't address certain issues or you are left with lingering questions, I would very much like to hear about that as well.

You can leave your comments directly on my website by completing my feedback form or send me an email at ronika@montrealfinancial.ca.

Connect with Me

I would love for us to connect, which you can do by subscribing to my biweekly newsletter, where I discuss topics of interest to small businesses, provide tax and QuickBooks tips, and links to my latest articles. You can also email me at ronika@montrealfinancial.ca.

INTRODUCTION

When starting a new for-profit business in Canada, you have two choices – you can simply register your business as a sole proprietorship or partnership, or you can incorporate. Over the years, many small business owners have come to me looking for guidance on what type of business structure is best for their situation and once this decision has been made, the essential information they need to know about accounting and tax.

My goal in writing this book to provide this guidance in a way that is accessible to anyone who is planning to start a new corporation. There are many types of businesses that decide to incorporate – you might be in the startup phase and feel that a corporation is best suited to your needs. You might have outgrown your unincorporated business and want to transition. Or you might be an independent contractor who is required to incorporate or wants to maximize the tax planning opportunities afforded by a corporation.

This book takes you through every step of the process of starting your corporation and provides you with the knowledge that will allow you to run your business smoothly, right from the outset.

This book is divided up into the following sections:

Incorporation explores what you need to consider prior to incorporating your business, decisions you will need to make when starting your corporation (whether you do it yourself or have someone else do it for you), and the factors to consider if you are transitioning your sole proprietorship to a new corporation.

Accounting reviews what new corporate owners should know about setting up bank accounts, the type of reports and accounting concepts that each new business owner should understand, why you should use accounting software, and what to look for in an accountant.

Tax examines the different tax obligations you must fulfill after starting your business, including sales tax, payroll/dividends, and corporate tax. Additionally, there is section that reviews options for investing excess funds within a corporation.

NAVIGATION

This book includes a variety of specialized terms that are commonly abbreviated, and some symbols to direct your attention to especially important or useful notes.

Acronyms

- CRA = Canada Revenue Agency (Revenue Canada)
- RQ = Revenue Quebec
- GST = Goods and Services Tax
- HST = Harmonized Sales Tax
- QST = Quebec Sales Tax
- DAS = Deductions at Source (amounts deducted from employee payroll)
- ITC = Input tax credit (GST/HST paid on expenses)

Text Boxes

Sometimes, it is useful to illustrate a point using an example.

> ❖ An ***EXAMPLE*** box illustrates the result of a procedure, a case study, or an illustration.

In addition, there are a number of different commentary boxes throughout the book.

> ⚠ An ***ALERT*** box contains a warning.

> ➢ A ***NOTE*** box contains a comment or a point for consideration.

> ✓ A ***TIP*** box suggests a way to work more efficiently or effectively.

PART 1: Incorporation

BEST PRACTICES FOR NEW CORPORATIONS

When starting your new corporation, there are certain best practices that you should implement to ensure that your corporation runs smoothly right from the beginning. This helps you to focus on your business and reduces the chances of receiving unpleasant letters from the government.

- Maintain all your incorporation documentation, either physically in a file folder or scan it to accounting/corporate folder on your computer. This will be very useful when you are asked for your corporate documentation, business numbers etc. by your business associates or CRA.

- Always read any documents that you receive from the government and determine if additional action is required. If you don't understand them, there is usually a number that you can call to get more information. Avoiding government notices does not make the problem go away and will usually make the situation worse.

- For many small corporations, not much needs to be done at the beginning in terms of accounting, sales tax, or corporate tax, as deadlines are often many months away. However, it is a good idea to set up your accounting system and to source an accountant. This will ensure that you are not scrambling at the last minute to meet deadlines and so avoid errors and/or penalties.

- If you register for payroll, filings usually need to be submitted monthly. It is important that you understand the deadlines and pay deductions on employees' salaries by the due date. If not, interest and penalties for late payroll deductions are steep.

- If you decide to borrow money from the corporation, ensure that have a plan to either repay it within one year or declare it as a salary or dividend. If not, CRA will assess it as income that will result in unnecessary taxes (and of course interest and penalties).

- Keep all your source documents: receipts, bills, expenses, and invoices. Ideally, scan your documents into an accounting folder that is organized so that you can access the documents easily. Alternatively, a physical filing system is also fine. Most accounting software will also allow you to attach the source documents to the transaction record.

- Ensure that you maintain enough funds in the corporation to pay your taxes. For GST/HST, remember that you are simply an agent of CRA. You collect these amounts on their behalf and pay them by a specific due date. These funds should not be used as cash flow in the business. It can be useful to open a separate savings account, where you transfer estimated sales tax payable; this also allows you to collect some interest.

- Be aware of tax deadlines, even if you have an accountant, and ensure that you give your accountant enough time to prepare and submit your tax filings.

- Most accounting and tax concepts relating to small business corporations are fairly straightforward. Since you know your business better than anyone, it is beneficial to understand these concepts so that you can better contribute to the decision-making process.

- Be disciplined with your business banking. Using personal bank accounts, beyond a handful of transactions, can lead to issues with CRA. If you do use personal bank accounts for a few transactions, create an expense report or a document trail.

- When claiming expenses, ensure that they are reasonable and relate to the business. Large amounts of expenses can raise red flags for CRA that can then lead to ongoing audits.

WHAT ARE THE DIFFERENT TYPES OF BUSINESS STRUCTURES IN CANADA?

Business Structures

When embarking on a new business venture, one of the first decisions that has to be made is the type of legal structure that best suits the needs of the new business. In Canada, there are essentially two choices:

- **Unincorporated** (Sole Proprietorship, Partnership)

  Registered businesses are simply an extension of the individual and as such the regulatory and tax obligations are relatively minimal. Setting up a small business is a fairly simple and inexpensive process. The business owner reports (and pays taxes on) the income from the business as part of the personal tax return. The owner is also responsible for the debts of the business.

- **Incorporated** (Corporation)

  A corporation is a legal entity where the owners (shareholders) are separate from the business. Setting up a corporation is more complex than a business registration. Decisions have to be made regarding the jurisdiction the corporation will be established in (Federal vs Provincial), who will serve as directors, what shareholders will own the corporation, what the share structure will be, and how the owner and/or officers will be remunerated. The corporation assumes the debt obligations and pays taxes at a corporate level. Finally, a corporation, being a separate legal "person", enjoys limited liability, which is defined by Revenue Canada as follows:

As a general rule, the shareholders of a corporation are not responsible for its debts. If the corporation goes bankrupt, a shareholder will not lose more than his or her investment (unless the shareholder has provided personal guarantees for the corporation's debts). Creditors also cannot sue shareholders for liabilities (debts) incurred by the corporation, even though shareholders are owners of the corporation. Note, however, that if a shareholder has another relationship with the corporation — for example, as a director — then he or she may, in certain circumstances, be liable for the debts of the corporation.

Which Structure Is Best?

Like many small business decisions, whether to register or
incorporate depends on the business owner's specific set of
circumstances. When deciding on which structure to use, there
are several questions that a small business owner should
consider:

1. **Does the new business venture need limited liability? Or
    will insurance be an adequate replacement?**

    A corporation creates a new legal entity that is distinct from
    the creator. As such, the liability of the company is limited
    to the shareholders' investment. (This does not apply in the
    case of personal guarantees or where directors have specific
    obligations etc.) This means that, in most cases, if a
    corporation is sued, its potential losses are limited to the
    assets of the corporation; the assets of the owner are not
    exposed to risk.

    > ⚠ *Note that there are some cases where director's liability
    > applies or where the corporate owner(s) is personally
    > liable for the debts of a corporation.*

2. **As the owner/shareholder of the corporation, are you able
    to leave funds in the business? Or will you need to
    withdraw all of the profits of the business for living
    expenses?**

    As a sole proprietorship you are simply taxed on the profits
    of the business at your personal tax rate. A corporation is
    also taxed on the profits of the business but at a lower
    corporate tax rate. You can you pay yourself a salary or
    dividend and the leave the remaining funds in the

corporation. These funds are then available to invest directly within the corporation.

3.   **Are you willing and able to spend money on incorporation costs and ongoing maintenance costs?**

There are costs relating to setting up a corporation and ongoing maintenance, including governmental, legal, and accounting fees that are usually higher than for a sole proprietorship.

4.   **Are you comfortable with the increased reporting requirements for a corporation, as you will mostly likely require the services of an accountant and possibly a lawyer?**

A separate set of legal and accounting records needs to be maintained. The accounting function is more involved, since the reporting required for the corporate tax return is more extensive and often requires actual accounting software rather than just a spreadsheet, which is what many unincorporated business owners use. Additionally, a corporation needs to file an Annual Return and a corporate Tax Return each year that is separate from each shareholder's personal Tax Return. Any changes to the corporation's structure, address, officers, etc. must be registered.

5.   **Do your clients, bank, or other stakeholders require that you incorporate? Or do you need the credibility associated with having a corporation?**

Certain business relationships may require the intermediary structure of a corporation, and "Inc.", "Limited", and "Corporation" all carry a certain social cachet.

6. **Do you have plans to build an enduring business that you might want to transfer upon your retirement or death?**

Because a sole proprietorship essentially IS the owner, the actual business ceases operations when the owner does (though assets may be sold/transferred). In contrast, a corporation can continue long after the original shareholders have sold or bequeathed their shares.

> ➢ **Note**: *Owners of small business shares benefit from a lifetime capital gains exemption of $866,912. This allows a shareholder to sell the shares of qualifying corporations tax-free for gains up to $866,000*
>
> ⇨ *Note also that this represents the full amount of the gain. The actual taxable capital gain is 50% of this amount: $433,456. The balance of $433,000 is non-taxable in the hands of the shareholder.*

Other Factors to Consider

1. **Lower Tax Rates:** Corporations, particularly small businesses, benefit from corporate tax rates that are lower than individual, personal tax rates.

> ➢ *Note that lower tax rates do not usually apply to incorporated rental properties and other types of investment-related businesses that generate passive income, unless you have 6 or more employees.*

2. **Jurisdiction:** If you do decide to incorporate, you will have to decide whether a Federal or Provincial corporation is more appropriate. A Federal corporation is more expensive; however, it provides heightened name protection and additional credibility and might make more sense if you are planning to operate your business across Canada and/or internationally.

3. **Owner Remuneration:** Owner-managed corporations need to determine the method and amount of remuneration. While registered business owners are simply taxed on the profits of the business, a corporation must pay salaries or dividends to its owners as employees or shareholders respectively.

> ➤ *Note that there are no restrictions on having employees whether you are registered or incorporated.*

4. **Access to Capital:** Corporations generally have more ways of raising capital, e.g., they can issue shares or sell bonds. Banks are often more comfortable lending to corporate entities with some established history. A corporation can be perceived as more professional than a sole proprietorship.

5. **Income Splitting:** Shares of corporations can be allocated among family members, allowing them to draw dividend income from the business. Keep in mind that the federal government targeted this type of tax planning and has imposed a set of criteria that evaluates the tax rate on dividends received by family members of business owners (Note: this does not apply to salaries). Although the rules are complex, the TOSI (tax on split income) legislation, introduced in 2018, essentially attempts to determine whether the shareholder is actively involved in the corporation, specifically younger shareholders, to ensure that owners are not trying to reduce their tax bills by allocating dividends to related taxpayers with much lower personal tax rates.

6. **Complex Structure and Taxation:** Corporations by their nature are more complex. Additionally, there are numerous tax considerations that can arise from corporate transactions including use of assets for personal reasons, transfer of assets to related parties, tax on capital, dividends to related family members (see above), etc.

7. **Losses:** Corporate losses remain within the corporation and cannot be transferred to the shareholder, whereas, with a sole proprietorship, losses, with certain exceptions, can be offset against other sources of income thereby reducing taxes payable. A corporation may however amalgamate with another corporation to utilize its losses.

8. **Growth:** Your business is experiencing growth that requires a more official business structure and a separate legal entity to deal with the additional complexities of growth.

9. **Adding A Partner**: You might decide that you want to add a partner to your business for which you need to create a new business structure.

10. **Taking Advantage of Loans, Incentives, Tax Credits:** It is usually easier for corporations to get certain types of grants, loans, incentives and tax credits.

11. **Set Up a Holdco:** When you set up a corporation to conduct your business activities, it is referred to as an operating company or Opco. In addition to your Opco, you can also set up a Holding Company or Holdco to own all or part of your corporation's shares to take advantage of advanced tax planning opportunities. Dividends can be paid to the Holdco that can then be used directly for investment in passive assets such as real estate or investments, or can be distributed to shareholders of the Holdco, with greater flexibility. For more insight into this subject, speak with your accountant.

If you determine that your business is still in its infancy and there are no issues relating to liability nor external requirements to incorporate, it might make sense to wait and see how the business evolves. A registered small business can decide to incorporate at any time. Alternatively, if after reviewing the above criteria, you assess that it is just a matter of time before you will need to incorporate, it might be better to do it right away.

CORPORATIONS WITH ONE CLIENT: EMPLOYEE VS SELF EMPLOYED

Sometimes a client will require that you set up a corporation to secure a contract with them rather than simply hiring you as an employee. In this type of situation, there is a risk that you might be deemed an employee by CRA. It is not enough for the person paying you to determine your classification since they may have other reasons for deeming you an independent contractor. Consequently, it is important to ensure that you fulfill at least some of the criteria listed below so that if you or your client are audited, you can demonstrate that you qualify as self employed. If audited, CRA will assess the facts of your situation and come up with a determination by reviewing the following:

Criteria to Determine Self Employment

- Do you have control over how the work is done, i.e., do you work independently without anyone overseeing your work?

- Do you have more than one client?

- Are you allowed to take on other clients without restrictions from your other clients?

- Can you decide to subcontract your work?

- Can you decline to do work?

- Do you provide your own tools and equipment - do you use your own computer, are you responsible for paying for software subscriptions, are you responsible for repair or replacement of your work tools if something breaks?

- Do you market yourself?

- Can you hire someone else to do the work without approval from someone else?

- Do you bear the risk and responsibility for the work done, i.e., if it is not done properly will you still get paid?

- Is there a written contract detailing the terms and conditions of the work?

- Do you invoice your client?

- Have you been hired for a specific job?

If you are able to answer in the affirmative to at least some of these questions, then you will be in a better position to defend yourself to CRA. Ideally, you would want to ensure that your agreement with your client is structured in a way that incorporates these criteria. If CRA denies your classification as self employed, they will deem your corporation to be a Personal Services Business which can lead to significant penalties and interest.

> ➤ *The distinction between employee and self employed is also important when you plan to hire workers in your corporation. You should review the criteria above to ensure that, if you are hiring a subcontractor, they meet the definition of self employed.*

What Are the Implications of Being a Self-Employed Owner vs an Employee?

There are several differences that, when faced with a choice between being an employee or an independent contractor, are important to understand:

- An employee often has certain entitlements including laws against wrongful dismissal, vacation and severance pay, and other perks including company contributions to health insurance, pension, and life insurance plans. Self employed workers, conversely, have to bear these risks and costs on their own.

- In addition to calculating, collecting, and remitting employee payroll taxes, employers are required to pay additional taxes for their employees. Self-employed individuals are responsible for calculating and remitting their own taxes.

- Employees are entitled to employment insurance benefits, whereas business owners are usually not eligible (unless they sign up for a special program which only has limited benefits).

- The self employed are allowed to claim certain business-related deductions against their income, including home office expenses, automobile expenses, and telephone costs, thereby reducing their income taxes. Employees may be entitled to these types of deductions but on a more restricted basis.

- If is often easier for employees to get loans, mortgages, and credit cards as they are perceived as having greater income stability. Self employed workers often have uneven income streams and a greater risk of collection, which can impact negatively on their ability to get credit.

Although, there is more effort, risk and responsibility that goes along with being self employed, there is also greater control, potential for profit and flexibility.

HOW TO START YOUR CORPORATION

The very idea of a corporation can be intimidating, but the vast majority of business corporations in Canada are small businesses, many operated entirely by one person. You can set-up your own corporation, or you can obtain assistance from specialists in filing the necessary documents with the government. Regardless of which way you choose to establish the corporation, you will have to make the same decisions.

Where to Incorporate: Federal or Provincial

You have two options when incorporating your business: you can either incorporate Federally (Canada corporation) or you can incorporate at the Provincial level (e.g., Ontario corporation), generally in the province in which you are a resident.

The choice between whether to incorporate Federally vs Provincially depends on your goals for the corporation.

Benefits of a Federal Corporation

- If your plans for your business are Canada-wide rather than simply providing goods or services in your province, then a Federal corporation gives you more flexibility.

> ✓ *If you are planning to start an e-commerce business where you will be selling within Canada and internationally, you are better off choosing a Federal corporation. Conversely, if you are an independent contractor that simply needs a corporation to invoice their local clients, a provincial corporation is probably adequate.*

- A Federal corporation gives you a certain additional amount of name protection Canada-wide, since when you register a corporation, you are also registering a name.

- If you think that you might move to another province in the future, it is much easier to transition a Federal corporation than a Provincial one.

Benefits of a Provincial Corporation

- Federal corporations require at least one Canadian resident director, while some provinces do not have this requirement. As such, if you are a non-resident or planning to become one, you might choose a Provincial corporation.

- Establishing a Provincial corporation is typically cheaper than a Federal corporation. If you establish a Federal corporation, you will also be required to register that corporation in a Province. This typically requires a registration fee in addition to the original incorporation fee. This means that establishing a Federal corporation could be twice as expensive as establishing a Provincial corporation. Various administrative filings can have associated fees as well; these are doubled when a corporation is Federal.

- Because Provincial corporations only interact with one level of government regarding their governance, there is less administrative paperwork. Provincial corporations must file an Annual Return; Federal corporations must file a Federal Annual Return and usually a Provincial Annual Return as well.

> ⚠ *Note that an Annual Return is different from a corporate tax return. It is a common area of confusion and causes many corporation owners to ignore their Annual Return filing since they think their accountants are taking care of it. You should verify this with your accountant.*
>
> ⚠ *Failing to submit your required Annual Return can lead to the automatic dissolution or deregistration of your corporation. There are significant fees involved in correcting this problem.*

Quebec

- Both Federal and Provincial corporations require that you file tax returns at the Federal and Provincial level. Tax software tends to integrate both the Federal and Provincial tax regulations, so this is usually not an issue, except for Quebec. If you incorporate in Quebec, it is important for you (or your accountant) to have an understanding of Quebec-based tax rules.

How to Choose a Corporate Name

Every corporation must have a name that legally identifies it. This is one of the biggest decisions in the process and worth spending some time considering. You probably already have some ideas, but there are both requirements and restrictions that apply.

A corporation may have either a **numbered name** or a **word name**, but before we discuss those, let's look at the **legal ending**.

Legal Ending

All corporations will have a legal ending as part of their name that indicates publicly that the enterprise is a corporation. For Canada corporations, there are three choices:

- Incorporated (or Inc.)
- Limited (or Ltd.)
- Corporation (or Corp.)

> ➢ *The French versions "Incorporée", "Limitée" (or "Ltée"), and "Société par actions de régime federal" (or "S.A.R.F.") are also valid for Canada corporations.*

All three are functionally the same; there is no legal or practical difference between an Inc. and a Ltd. in Canada. The legal ending in other countries can mean different things.

> ➢ *Inc. is more common in the United States, Ltd. in the United Kingdom, and Corp. globally.*

Choose whichever one best suits you. The sound of how your name combines with your legal ending is a perfectly valid consideration.

> ⚠ *"Incorporated" and "Inc." are not interchangeable! If your company is named 12345678 Canada Inc., you may not use the name 12345678 Canada Incorporated.*

Numbered Name

Companies that are not public-facing, such as holding companies, or that do not require a distinctive name, are often set up as a **numbered name** corporation. This is the simplest choice and also usually the fastest to have approved. A numbered name will consist of three components:

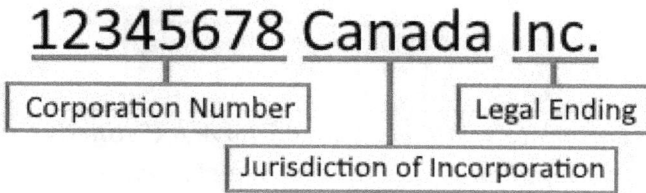

12345678 Canada Inc.

| Corporation Number | | Legal Ending |

| | Jurisdiction of Incorporation | |

Corporation Number

This is assigned automatically by the government agency. You may not choose the number. All corporations, numbered name and word name, have a corporation number; in the case of a numbered name corporation, your number is your name. Your corporation number will be the next one available in the series and will form the distinctive and unique component of your corporate name.

Jurisdiction of Incorporation

This is determined by where you choose to incorporate your business. If you establish a Federal corporation, this will be "Canada". If you choose a Provincial corporation, this will be the province you incorporate in, e.g., "Ontario".

> ✓ *A numbered name corporation may also **register** a name to use for business purposes. This is frequently referred to as a **DBA** for **Doing Business As**. This name does not enjoy the same protections as a corporate name.*

Word Name

Most people starting a new corporation will choose a word name. Word names also have three components:

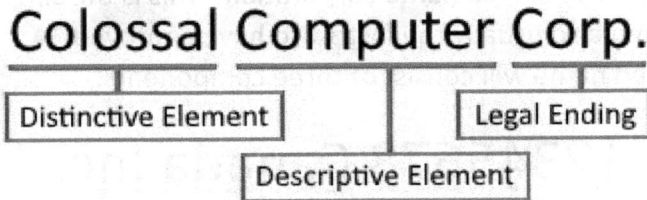

Colossal Computer Corp.

| Distinctive Element | | Legal Ending |

| Descriptive Element |

> ✓ A corporate word name MUST have a **distinctive element** and a **legal ending**; a **descriptive element** is highly recommended but not mandatory.

Distinctive Element

The distinctive element is the unique part of your corporate name, and the one that expresses the personality or the character of the business.

The distinctive element of your corporate word name can be:

- your personal name, first or last or other (e.g., Smith or John),
- a geographic/regional word (e.g., Canada, Windsor, Vancouver, Manitoba),
- a descriptive word (e.g., Superior, Discount, Elite),
- a general word (e.g., Blueberry, Bulldog, Sunset),
- or a made-up word (e.g., Schmoogle, MacroComp).

A word name may include letters, symbols, and numbers.

> ❖ EXAMPLE: "#1 A+ Cut Above Corp."

You can also choose a phrase for your distinctive element that combines the different types of words to produce a name.

> ❖ *EXAMPLE: "Bright Star Toronto Inc."*

Choosing the distinctive element is the hardest and most personal part of the process—and the one you choose may not be approved! Be ready by having a shortlist of possible names that you feel comfortable using.

Descriptive Element

The descriptive element is more technical. This is a word or phrase that describes the type of product you will make, the service you will provide, or the industry that you will be part of.

> ❖ **Examples**:
>
> - Video   - Services
> - Management   - Enterprises
> - Furniture   - Restaurant
> - Technology   - Consulting

This descriptive element is added to the Distinctive element and the legal ending.

> ❖ *EXAMPLE: Bright Star **Tutoring Services** Ltd.*

> ✓   *Typically, corporate word names that contain a descriptive element are easier to have approved.*

Word Name Restrictions

Not every name proposed will be accepted by the governing authority.

New and Original

The first and most important requirement is that your name must be distinctive and cannot create confusion with other names or trademarks. The upside of this is that, once your name is approved, other people will not be able to establish businesses that create confusion with yours. This is one of the reasons to incorporate in the first place.

> ⚠ *Corporate word names consisting only of a personal name or a geographic word plus a legal ending (e.g., John Smith Inc. or Toronto Ltd.) will rarely if ever be approved. Make sure to add a **descriptive element** if you are using a personal name or a geographic word! (E.g., John Smith Computers Inc. or Toronto Distillers Ltd.)*

Prohibited Terms

The governing authority may also restrict other specific terms. In general, avoid words that:

- suggest official government support or relationships,
- suggest institutional support or relationships (e.g., with a bank or university),
- mislead the public in any way about your product or service, such as where or how it is made,
- are offensive.

❖ *EXAMPLE:*

For a Federal corporation, a corporate name will not be approved if it contains the following:

- *"Parliament Hill" or "Colline du Parlement",*
- *"Royal Canadian Mounted Police", "RCMP", "Gendarmerie royale du Canada", or "GRC",*
- *"United Nations", "UN", "Nations Unies", or "ONU" (where a relationship with the United Nations is suggested),*
- *any word considered obscene.*

Language

Depending on the jurisdiction in which your incorporate, the governing authority may have specific requirements or restrictions regarding the language of your word name.

❖ *EXAMPLE 1:*

A Federal corporation word name may be in:

    - English only: **Colossal Computer Ltd.**

    - French only: **Ordinateur Colossal Ltée**

    - both English and French versions:

Colossal Computer Ltd. / Ordinateur Colossal Ltée.

    - English and French combined:

Ordinateur Colossal Computer Ltd.

❖ *EXAMPLE 2:*

A Quebec corporation word name MUST be in French. The **distinctive element** *MAY be in English, but the* **descriptive element** *MUST then be in French.*

The rules are a little different for Federal corporations that are registered in Quebec (as compared with Quebec corporations).

It is important to verify the requirements in the jurisdiction where you plan to incorporate.

Word Name Searches

Once you have decided on a corporate word name, it is time to do a **corporate name search**. There are different procedures for performing a name search depending on the jurisdiction you are incorporating in.

In general, a corporate name search will reveal whether there are already corporate names similar to yours active in your jurisdiction. Using computer search technology, the governing authority will check various databases to determine if your name is identical with or similar to any already existing corporate entities. A nominal fee is charged per name searched.

You will receive a copy of the results of this search, typically in the form of a list containing similar or related names and some other information, including date of incorporation and location of the registered office.

Performing a name search is **mandatory** in some jurisdictions, and **optional** in others.

> ➤ *A* _NUANS_ *name search is mandatory for Canada and Ontario corporations; a corporate name search is optional in Quebec.*

Corporate Name Success

As mentioned above, the key to getting a corporate word name approved by the governing authority is ensuring that it is:

1. Distinctive
2. Original
3. Not Prohibited

Before spending time and money on name searches, use your preferred search engine and perform some Internet searches for the names that you have in mind. If you find the identical name already in use, then it is time to come up with another one. You can also make use of the Federal and various Provincial enterprise databases for these free searches.

❖ *EXAMPLE:*

♦ *You may search for Canada corporations* here.
♦ *You may search for Ontario corporation IN PERSON at Central Production and Verification Services Branch Public Office in Toronto.*
♦ *You may search for Quebec corporations* here.

These searches are an excellent starting point. You may find that the name you want is already taken, but that a variation is available. Also, you may be inspired by some of the names you find and choose a whole new direction.

Typically, a longer, more specific name will enjoy more success at the approval stage than a shorter, more general name—many of these have already been taken. Balancing the various elements and doing your homework will smooth your way to a corporate word name that you're happy to use.

How to Set-Up Your Corporate Structure

The next decision you have to make concerns the organization of your corporation. Answer the following questions:

- Who will own shares of the corporation?
- Will different owners have different types of shares?
- Who will control the corporation as voting shareholders?
- How many Directors will the corporation have?

Corporate Shares

A **share** in a corporation is a virtual "piece" of the business, owned by an individual person (or sometimes by a group of other people, sometimes organized as another corporation) called the **shareholder**.

There are a variety of different types (called "classes") of shares, but we will only deal with the basics, **Common** shares and **Preferred** shares.

The type of share owned by a shareholder will give that shareholder certain rights and responsibilities.

Common Shares

The standard type of share, and the one your corporation will have if you choose to have only one class of share, Common shares grant the shareholder:

- the right to vote,
- the right to receive dividends (if declared by the Board of Directors), and
- the right to receive the remaining property of the corporation should it be dissolved.

Additional rights may be granted to holders of Common shares, but the above three are standard.

If your business will have only one owner, this is the only type of share you need. Similarly, if you will have more than one owner, but you want all owners treat more or less the same, even if the proportion of ownership is different, then Common shares are appropriate.

> ❖ *EXAMPLE:*
>
> *If you go into business with a partner, you may choose to each hold 50% of the Common shares, and each time a dividend is issued, you would each receive 50% of it.*
>
> *Alternatively, you might have major and minor partners, where A holds 40% of the Common shares, B hold 35%, C holds 20%, and the very minor partner D holds 5%.*

Preferred Shares

Preferred shares may or may not be accompanied by the right to vote and/or the right to receive the corporation's remaining property after dissolution. Most typically, Preferred shares grant the shareholder the right to receive dividends **before** dividends are paid to the holders of Common shares (hence Preferred).

When a dividend is declared for Common shares, all holders of Common shares will receive an amount of the total in proportion to their number of Common shares relative to the total number.

In contrast, a dividend issued to holders of Preferred shares will be divided up only among the holders of the class of Preferred share named when the dividend is issued.

> ❖ *EXAMPLE:*
>
> *If a dividend of $1000.00 is declared for Common shares, and there are 10 shareholders each with 10 Common shares, each shareholder will receive $100.00.*

> ◆   *EXAMPLE, cont.*
>
> *However, if 2 of those shareholders are also holders of Preferred shares, say 50 each, and a dividend is declared for Preferred shares of $1000.00, each of the 2 Preferred shareholders would receive $500.00 while the Common shareholders would receive $0.00.*

Preferred shares are commonly used in order to issue dividends to specific individuals rather than to everyone who holds shares in the corporation.

> ✓   *Your share structure is not written in stone. As your corporation grows and changes, you may wish to change the types of shares that your corporation can issue. There are some technicalities and costs involved, but you are allowed to make these changes after you incorporate, if you need to.*

Restrictions on Share Transfers

You may choose to limit the how, when, and why shareholders may sell or transfer their shares to someone else. There are a vast number of possible considerations here, most of which do not apply to small business corporations.

> ❖ *EXAMPLE:*
>
> *If you have established a corporation with a partner, you may include a clause as a Restriction on Share Transfers that requires a shareholder wishing to sell shares to offer the first to the other shareholder, and the terms of such a sale. This would prevent one partner from leaving the business and yoking the other founder with a stranger.*

Board of Directors

Once you know who will own the corporation, and what rights those different owners will have, it's time to make some decisions about the Board of Directors.

The Board of Directors is the controlling body of the corporation. This doesn't mean that the Directors do the day-to-day work of the corporation, but rather that the Board makes the Big Decisions, like who will run the corporation day-to-day, and when money will be moved out of the corporation to the shareholders.

You will decide how many Directors will sit on the Board, in terms of a minimum (of at least one) and a maximum. The Directors are elected by the shareholders, typically at the Annual General Meeting. Some may be appointed by the holders of Preferred shares, but that sort of consideration is beyond the scope of this book.

> ✓ *It is common for small business corporations to have one shareholder (the owner), one employee (the owner), and one director (the owner). This may seem strange, but remember that corporations can be big or small, and the same basic legal structure applies to them all.*

Restrictions on Business Activities

Some corporations are formed for one purpose—and one purpose alone. Others may be focussed in only one sector of the economy but provide different types of services or products—or products and services—in that sector. Others may be generalists.

You will get to decide whether your corporation will be limited in any way in terms of the business activities it may engage in.

You may set any restriction you like—or none at all.

> ➢ *Unless you decide to restrict the activities of your*
>   *corporation, you are free to conduct as many types of*
>   *business activity as you like. You may have a computer*
>   *software corporation and also use it to sell honey at the*
>   *farmer's market on the weekend.*

Other Provisions

The final consideration before you begin the incorporation process is whether there is anything else that you want to make official right from the start with your corporation.

This is a catch-all area for any restriction, requirement, or piece of official business not covered in the previous sections.

How to Get Incorporated

Once you have made the above decisions, you are ready to begin the actual process of incorporation.

DIY

Incorporating a business is something you can do yourself. Most jurisdictions offer an Internet portal that will enable you to go through the different steps in order to produce your Articles of Incorporation—the founding document of your corporation.

> ⚠ *If you establish a Federal corporation, you will also be*
>   *required to **register** it in the province where the*
>   *corporation is established. This can require an additional*
>   *fee and sometimes the use of a different, Provincial*
>   *Internet portal.*

The above sections will provide the information you need to enter during the incorporation process. The chief advantage of this option is that you pay only the direct fees charged by the governing authorities; the chief disadvantage is the stress and uncertainty about making sure you did everything correctly. Doing it yourself is best reserved for very simple incorporations.

Links to Incorporate

Use the following links to incorporate in each jurisdiction:

Canada

https://www.ic.gc.ca/app/scr/cc/CorporationsCanada/bs/crp-wz.html

Alberta

https://www.alberta.ca/incorporate-alberta-corporation.aspx#jumplinks-2

British Columbia

https://www2.gov.bc.ca/gov/content/employment-business/business/managing-a-business/permits-licences/businesses-incorporated-companies/incorporated-companies

Manitoba

https://companiesoffice.gov.mb.ca/forms_mbcorporations.html

New Brunswick

https://www2.gnb.ca/content/gnb/en/services/services_renderer.201
448.Incorporation_Registration_of_a_Business_-
_Business_Corporations_Act.html

Newfoundland and Labrador

https://www.gov.nl.ca/dgsnl/registries/companies/corp-inc/

Northwest Territories

https://www.justice.gov.nt.ca/en/nwt-corporations/

Nova Scotia

https://beta.novascotia.ca/incorporate-limited-company

Nunavut

http://nunavutlegalregistries.ca/cr_index_en.shtml

Ontario

https://www.ontario.ca/page/incorporating-business-corporation

Prince Edward Island (couldn't find a good PEI page)

https://ocbr.princeedwardisland.ca/ocbr/login

Saskatchewan

https://www.isc.ca/CorporateRegistry/Forms/Pages/Business-Corporations-Act-Forms.aspx

Yukon

https://yukon.ca/en/incorporate-yukon-business-corporation

Links to Register

If you established a Federal (Canada) corporation, you will also need to register it in your province of residence.

> ✓ *If your business will be registered in Ontario, Newfoundland and Labrador, or Nova Scotia, you can do this as part of the Federal incorporation.*

Also, if you operate a Federal or Provincial corporation based in one province, there are circumstances when you may be required to register in another.

Use the following links to register in each jurisdiction:

Alberta

https://www.alberta.ca/register-out-of-province-corporation.aspx

British Columbia

https://www2.gov.bc.ca/gov/content/employment-
business/business/managing-a-business/permits-
licences/businesses-incorporated-companies/incorporated-
companies#extraprovincial

Manitoba

https://companiesoffice.gov.mb.ca/forms_extraprovincialcorporations
.html

New Brunswick

https://www2.gnb.ca/content/gnb/en/services/services_renderer.201
448.Incorporation___Registration_of_a_Business_-
_Business_Corporations_Act.html

Newfoundland and Labrador

https://www.gov.nl.ca/dgsnl/registries/companies/corp-art-inc/

Northwest Territories

https://www.justice.gov.nt.ca/en/files/extraterritorial-
corporations/Guide%20ET%20Reg/HOW%20TO%20Extra%20Territorial
ly%20Register.en.pdf

Nova Scotia

https://beta.novascotia.ca/register-extra-provincial-federal-or-foreign-
corporation

Nunavut

http://nunavutlegalregistries.ca/cr_index_en.shtml

Ontario

https://www.ontario.ca/page/extra-provincial-corporations-doing-
business-ontario

Prince Edward Island

https://ocbr.princeedwardisland.ca/ocbr/login

Saskatchewan

https://www.isc.ca/CorporateRegistry/RegisteringaBusiness/Registery
ourBusiness/RegisteraNWPorEPBusiness/Pages/default.aspx

Yukon

https://yukon.ca/en/register-extra-territorial-business-corporation

Service Provider

There are a variety of paralegal services that will either assist you or complete the incorporation on your behalf. This is more expensive than doing it on your own, but you will benefit from the expertise and experience of the service provider, which can often save you time and perhaps avoid costly errors. For basic and moderately complex incorporations, a service provider is often a convenient option.

> ✓ *I recommend INCORP to my clients. Their full-service approach and excellent pricing are the ideal fit for most entrepreneurs launching a new corporation.*

Lawyer

If your incorporation is sufficiently complex, with many different classes of shares and an elaborate structure, a lawyer will be the best choice—though also the most expensive! In most cases, a lawyer is overkill.

THE CORPORATE YEAR END AND HOW TO CHOOSE ONE

A year end represents the completion of an accounting period, which is typically one year. A sole proprietorship generally has a year end date that is consistent with the calendar year: December 31st for tax purposes. A corporation, conversely, can have a year end date that is any date in the year. Once you have selected your year end date, this will continue to be your year end for administrative, accounting, and tax purposes—unless you decide to change it. If you do decide to change it, you will need to complete and submit forms to the governing authority where you incorporated and the tax authorities, along with a valid reason for the change.

How to Select a Year End for a Corporation

A natural year end for any business, at first glance, would appear to be December 31st. However, this is not necessarily the best choice for a corporation. There are several reasons you might want to select a different year end for a corporation:

- Since the majority of companies have a year end on December 31st, it can be difficult to find an accountant who can give you their undivided attention. Busy season for corporate accountants tends to run between February and June, which is the period in which tax filings from December 31st need to be submitted and completed.

- Businesses that are seasonal might choose a year end that corresponds to the end of their busy season to ensure that the administrative work relating to the year end only needs to be done when the business owners and employees have more time available.

> ❖ *Example: Businesses that have inventory are generally required to do a physical count at year end. Choosing a year end that corresponds to a slow period makes this process significantly less burdensome.*

- Choosing a year end other than December 31st allows for tax deferral opportunities. Since any withdrawals from the corporation only have to be declared after the fiscal year end, you can defer dividend income to the calendar year in which your year ends. The same logic can be applied to bonuses, which can be paid up to 6 months after they are declared and shown as expenses for the corporation. Additionally, no instalments have to be paid until after your first-year end, which can help with cash flow.

> ❖ *For example, if you have a fiscal year end of March 31, 2022, but you have withdrawn funds from the corporation in 2021, you only have to declare these withdrawals as dividends in the 2022 calendar year.*

- CRA allows you to choose a fiscal year that is 53 weeks after your incorporation date. By extending the year end as long as possible after the incorporation date, you can save on accounting and tax preparation fees.

> ❖ *If your incorporation date is November 26th, 2021, you could choose a year end that is on October 31st, 2022 rather than December 31, 2021. By doing this, you can defer tax preparation fees to after October 31, 2022 when your tax filings start to come due.*

- If you have a subsidiary, parent, or sister corporation, it might make sense to choose a year end that corresponds to the associated corporation to make reporting easier.

What Are the Implications of Your Year End?

- Your year end will determine your tax filing and payment deadlines. Corporate tax returns are generally due within 6 months of the year end while sales tax filings are due within 3 months (assuming you are registered for annual sales tax filings). The year end also informs your instalment payment dates.

- The vast majority of businesses choose a year end that is the last day of a month. This makes a variety of accounting functions easier and allows for consistency in reporting.

- Year end dates also impact reporting to other entities besides revenue agencies including banks, shareholders, board of directors etc. In these cases, you would want to choose a year end where your company is most likely to meet conditions and covenants imposed by these entities.

> ✓ *A bank might require a certain debt to equity ratio. Choosing a year end in the month that you expect to have the strongest cash flow and are able to repay some debt could ensure that you meet the condition.*

CORPORATE MAINTENANCE

Because a corporation is a distinct legal "person", certain tasks must be performed, and paperwork must be filed with the relevant governing authorities on a regular basis in order to keep it "alive".

Annual Meetings

Corporations are required to hold two meetings on an annual basis: the Annual General Meeting of the Shareholders (AGM) and the Annual Meeting of the Directors (ADM).

> ✓ *In the case of a small business corporation, especially ones with one shareholder, it is common to simply write resolutions "in lieu" of holding a meeting with only one person.*

Annual General Meeting of the Shareholder(s)

The AGM is where the Director(s) report to the Shareholder(s) about the state of the corporation.

At a minimum, the following issues must be addressed at the AGM:

12. appoint an auditor (or waive the appointment of an auditor),
13. elect the director(s), and
14. consider the corporation's financial statements.

It is also appropriate to note major strategic decisions and financial events at the AGM. Minutes of the meeting must be kept and made available to the governing authority on request.

> ➤ *Minutes of the AGM are not required to be submitted to the government as a matter of routine.*

Annual Meeting of the Director(s)

The directors direct the activities of the corporation. They are high level administrators and meet on an occasional basis. In a small corporation, the chief function of the director(s) at the ADM is to appoint the corporation's **officers**. Officers perform the day-to-day operations of the corporation, and typically include the President, the Secretary, and the Treasurer.

> ✓   *In a small business corporation, one person may be the President, the Secretary, and the Treasurer all at once.*

Establishing a bank account typically requires an Officer to visit the bank and set things up.

Meetings of the ADM must be kept by the corporation's Secretary.

> ➤   *Minutes of the ADM are not required to be submitted to the government as a matter of routine.*

Annual Return

The Annual Return is a report filed by the corporation with the relevant government (Federal, Provincial, or both) about the activities of the corporation over the preceding year.

Typically, changes in the corporation's directors (but not its officers), its address, and its status as a distributing corporation must be reported. In addition, the date of the most recent AGM is reported.

> ⚠   *Failure to file the corporation's Annual Return, usually for two or more years, can result in the dissolution of the corporation by the governing authority. Re-activating the corporation can be as expensive as the initial incorporation, so make sure that you stay caught up!*

FROM SOLE PROPRIETORSHIP TO CORPORATION

When starting your new business, it often makes sense to choose the simplest structure, which is the sole proprietorship. This allows you to test the viability of your business idea and to see if the lifestyle and the related stress that goes along with being a business owner suits your personality and is in line with your long-term goals. Additionally, you might want to keep everything simple and not add any unnecessary complexity. Registering and maintaining a sole proprietorship is fairly straightforward; many business owners don't put much thought into the financial aspects of it until tax time. With a corporation the level of complexity and commitment increases.

There are several reasons that you might decide to transition your sole proprietorship to a corporation – please refer to the chapter on why you should incorporate.

Steps to Take When Transitioning from a Sole Proprietorship to a Corporation

1. Establish Your New Corporation

Please refer to section on how to start your corporation.

2. Register for New Sales Tax Numbers and Payroll Numbers

Please refer to section on registering for sales taxes and payroll.

3. Cancel Your Sole Proprietorship and Tax Numbers

Determine if you want to dissolve your current sole proprietorship or keep it running as an inactive business for a little while in case you would like to use it in the future for another business. You should however cancel your sole proprietorship sales tax and payroll numbers, if applicable, to avoid having to file $0 returns and incur potential penalties if these are not filed on time.

> ⚠ *If you want your corporation to have the same name as your sole proprietorship had, you will have to EITHER cancel your sole proprietorship **before** incorporating OR file a signed letter stating that you own the name and are transitioning to a corporation.*

4. Close Your Sole Proprietorship Bank Account and Open a New Corporate Bank Account

Close your business bank account for the sole proprietorship and set up a new bank account for the corporation. You can continue to use the business credit card, although it is better to get a corporate credit card, if possible.

5. Consider a Section 85 Rollover

When transitioning your existing unincorporated business to a corporation, you should consider whether you need to do a Section 85 rollover, which is a way of transferring assets from the sole proprietorship to the corporation. This is especially important if you have built a brand, or a customer list and your current business has some intangible value in addition to real assets such inventory and equipment. The purpose of a Section 85 rollover is to assess a value for the assets of the existing business, including intangibles, and transfer them over at their original cost so that you don't have to pay tax on capital gains.

> ⚠ *Many small business owners don't do a Section 85 rollover, which can be problematic if CRA decides that your business did have value upon transfer; the CRA may consequently assess tax.*

This article explains a Section 85 rollover in greater detail.

6. Change Contracts, Billing Etc. in Favour of the New Corporation

If you have contracts with customers/clients that you will be moving over the new corporation, make sure that these are updated to reflect the new entity and any other associated changes.

7. Get an Accountant

A corporation has greater complexity when it comes to tax reporting and preparation. As such, it is a good idea to find an accountant as soon as possible to help guide you through your obligations and let you know what you need to do right at the beginning to ensure a smooth transition.

8. Transition Your Accounting

Since a corporation is a separate legal entity, it is best practice to start a new accounting file. Some business owners continue to use the same accounting file, which can result in confusion particularly for tax purposes since tax reporting for a sole proprietorship is different than a corporation. A corporation's reporting starts on the date of incorporation; however, you might have transactions that relate to the sole proprietorship that overlap while you effect the transition.

Ideally, you should close out the current accounting software for your sole proprietorship. Make sure to export all relevant reports and data since inception of your business, before deprecating your account, including:

- balance sheets by fiscal year
- profit loss by fiscal year
- general ledger since inception
- trial balance by fiscal year
- accounts payable details
- accounts receivable details
- supplier, customer, employee lists
- sales tax details
- payroll details

PART 2: ACCOUNTING

SETTING UP A SEPARATE BANK AND CREDIT CARD ACCOUNT

Once you incorporate, you will receive a business number from CRA. This will allow you to set up a separate bank account for your corporation, which is one of the essential first steps after you have incorporated.

Why You Need to Have a Separate Corporate Bank Account

Since a corporation is a separate legal entity, a separate bank account that is in the name of the corporation is necessary to distinguish personal transactions from corporation transactions. Any transactions that go through your personal bank accounts are considered to be personal in nature. As such, even though you might have a corporation, if you are receiving invoice payments through your personal account, you will be taxed on these amounts as an individual taxpayer.

Other Advantages of a Business Bank Account

Stay Organized

Setting up a separate bank account when you start your business is one of the easiest tools available to organize your finances. For those of us who procrastinate and leave administrative tasks such as accounting to the end of the year or even closer to tax time, a bank account that is solely used for business transactions can be invaluable in assessing where you stand with respect to your finances at any given time. By referring to the balance in your bank account, you have a good idea of how much cash you have to spend on your business and how much you have available to pay yourself. Although unincorporated business owners do not technically pay themselves a salary for tax purposes (they are taxed on the total profit earned from the business - amounts withdrawn to pay yourself are not considered expenses), it is a good way to discipline yourself as you can limit how much you withdraw to a fixed monthly amount, while any excess funds are used to develop your business.

Separate Business from Personal

Another important to reason to have a separate bank account for your small business is to ensure the separation of business from personal transactions. In the event of an audit of your small business, the revenue agencies are likely to ask for your bank statements. Providing them with statements that combine personal and business banking will at a minimum lead to probing questions about non-business-related deposits and expenses. At worst, this could result in them assessing you on amounts received that are not business income, or they could disallow expenses. A separate bank account avoids this potential problem.

Avoid Manual Data Entry

Online accounting software like QuickBooks Online and Xero allow you to download your banking transactions automatically, which helps to reduce manual data entry of transactions and also ensures that all business related transactions are captured.

Conveniently Pay Business Taxes

A separate business bank account allows you to pay business taxes using online banking including sales tax, payroll taxes, and corporate income tax.

Capture All Business Transactions

Having a dedicated bank account that is reconciled on a regular basis (i.e., all entries on the bank statement are matched to your accounting records) ensures that you properly claim your expense deductions and ensures that you don't understate your invoices.

What Are the Limitations of a Separate Bank Account?

It's Not an Accounting System

A bank account, while helpful for understanding cash flow, does not replace an accounting system that would provide you with information on how much your customers owe you or how much you owe your suppliers.

Does not Provide Info on Outstanding Transactions

While the bank balance at the end of the period might give you some indication of profitability, it is far from exact. Additionally, it does not give you information on cheques that you have issued but that have not yet been cashed nor on deposits that may have been received but not yet processed.

Additional Fees

Fees charged by banks on business accounts can be high depending on the type of account that you have. On the plus side, these expenses are deductible from business income.

What Do You Need to Set Up a Business Bank Account?

When setting up a business bank account for a new corporation, the following documents are necessary:

- Certificate of Incorporation, Articles of Incorporation, or Articles of Amalgamation
- Registered Office and Board of Directors form
- Trade name registration (if applicable)

- A copy of the resolution directing the officers of the corporation to establish a bank account at that particular branch
- CRA business number (print a copy of the record for your corporation by searching it here)

The above documents will be made available to you after incorporation either through Industry Canada (or the province in which you incorporate) or through the agent that did the incorporation for you.

Why You Should Also Have a Separate Credit Card for Your Business

While it isn't as essential to have a separate credit card for your corporation, it is considered to be a best practice that helps you avoid issues with revenue agencies.

If you are not able to get a corporate credit card (many business owners experience resistance from the bank when starting their corporations as there is no credit history for the business), you should designate a personal credit card that you use exclusively for corporate expenses. This allows you deduct fees and interest charged on the credit card without having to prorate them based on business vs personal use.

Other reasons to have a separate credit card include:

Separate Business from Personal

A separate credit for your business can also be invaluable in helping to separate business from personal finances. It can also prevent personal transactions from showing up in your business accounting.

Don't Forget Business Deductions:

Many business owners tend to forget to deduct business expenses that are made on mixed use credit cards (the net result of which is higher taxes!).

Payments from Business Bank Account

Payments of your credit card balance should be made directly from your business bank account which gives you an even better separation of business vs personal and a more accurate picture of cash flow.

Other Factors to Consider When Opening a Bank Account

Most banks offer corporate accounts. Many business owners will simply choose the bank that they use for personal banking as the bank already knows them, which will make the process of setting up a new bank account a bit easier.

While simply choosing the bank that you already have a relationship with is fine, there are some other factors that you should consider:

- Does the bank have a program for small business owners?
- Do they offer credit facilities such as lines of credits or loan programs?
- What type of fees do they charge (keep in mind that bank fees are deductible for a corporation)?
- Do they have good customer service?
- Does the bank integrate with your accounting software, allowing you to download banking transactions automatically?
- Do they have locations that are easy to access, or, if they are virtual, is it easy to communicate with them?

- Do they have online banking and a mobile app that is easy to use?
- Can you make deposits through the mobile app?
- Are they offering any incentives for signing up?

WHAT TYPE OF ACCOUNTING REPORTS DO YOU NEED FOR A CORPORATION?

Financial Statements

A typical Financial Statement contains the following:

- Profit and Loss statement
- Balance Sheet
- Statement of Cash Flows
- Notes to the Financial Statements, which provide details for some of the line items on the Financial Statements and are generally prepared by accountants at the year end depending on your mandate with the accountant.

Profit and Loss

The accounting report that provides the best one-page perspective on your business, and which is vital for reporting your income to the government for tax purposes, is the **Profit and Loss statement**, which is also called an income statement. This report essentially summarizes your revenues and expenses by category. By deducting your expenses from your revenues (or total sales), you arrive at a net profit amount—or a net loss if your expenses exceed your sales.

There are three main sections on a simple profit and loss statement, though there may be more depending on the level of complexity.

- **Revenues** represent your total sales for the year. The categories for revenues can be whatever is most meaningful for your business. You can combine them all into one category or you can separate them out by type (products vs services) or region (Canada vs US) or source (website vs referral). With respect to tax reporting, there is usually only one line item that combines all your revenues.

- **Cost of Goods Sold** are the direct costs of selling your product and sometimes used for services if you have significant direct costs. These will include costs to purchase the raw materials or items that you sell, packaging of your product, shipping and duties, labels etc. They also include the cost of the labour to produce the goods. The change in inventory represents the cost of what you had available for sale at the beginning of the year vs your inventory at the end of the year.

- **Expenses** are generally those costs that you incur that indirectly relate to your business. The most significant of these expenses are usually salaries, rent, and advertising and marketing but can vary depending on your business.

Balance Sheet

The next report that is essential for all corporations and forms part of any business's Financial Statements is the **Balance Sheet**. This report shows a business's Assets, Liabilities, and Equity at a specific date. It is where you can see:

- How much money you have in your bank account
- Total amounts owing from Customers (Accounts Receivable)
- Inventory on hand
- Investments
- Fixed assets, such as furniture, equipment, and machinery
- Total amounts owing to Suppliers (Accounts Payable)
- Loans payable to shareholders

- Loans payable to third parties
- Share capital, which is how much the shareholders have contributed to the company
- Retained earnings, which is the accumulation of all earnings since inception of the business

Corporations require this report, minimally, at the year end date and I is useful to review regularly as it provides valuable information on what the corporation owns (assets), what the corporation owes (liabilities), and the net investment by the shareholders (equity), along with accumulated profits since inception.

> ➢ *The Total Assets on a Balance Sheet will also be equal to the Total Liabilities and Equity.*

Statement of Cash Flows

The **Statement of Cash Flows** (cash flow statement), while not necessary for tax reporting, can give you valuable insights into how much net cash is spent or generated by a business, focus on areas that need improvement and help plan for the future. A cash flow statement is typically broken down into three sections:

- **Operating activities** breaks down the cash inflows and outflow relating to the regular operations of the business.
- **Investing activities** breaks down the cash inflows and outflow relating to investments made and sold.
- **Financing activities** breaks down the cash inflows and outflow from financing activities such as loans or equity.

ACCOUNTING TERMS THAT EVERY BUSINESS OWNER SHOULD KNOW

When starting your business, you will be subjected to a great deal of financial jargon. This new vocabulary is important to know to help you get the most out of your accounting software. Additionally, you might be asked for financial information from your bank, CRA or RQ, suppliers, customers, and various other business partners. If you are unfamiliar with the terminology, then simple accounting and financial reporting becomes more difficult. Arming yourself with a basic vocabulary of the most common financial and accounting terms will help you develop a better understanding of your business and therefore be well equipped to answer any questions that come your way.

Accounts Receivable (A/R)

The accounting term for when customers owe you money is Accounts Receivable. This is also referred to as Customers Receivables or simply by its acronym: AR. If you have an accounting software where you enter your invoices to customers and corresponding payments, you will be able to produce what is known as an AR Aging Summary, which is a report that lists all the amounts that customers owe you, usually categorized in 30-day increments. The AR Aging Summary has the receivables that are the newest, referred to as current, in the first column. Each subsequent column is increased by 30 days i.e., current, 30 days, 60 days, 90 days, and then anything over 90 days is combined into one column. For example, a customer that you invoiced 2 months ago who has not yet paid you will show up under the 60 days heading. The older the account receivable, the more problematic it is, since there is a lower chance that it will be collected. It is important to know exactly which customers owe you money at any given time and follow up with them regularly to increase the chances of being paid. Anyone analyzing your business, such as a bank that is determining if you are creditworthy, will assess the age of the receivables and assign a lower value to them. Accounts Receivable are a Current Asset on your Balance Sheet.

Accounts Payable (A/P)

Similar to accounts receivable, Accounts Payable refers to the list of suppliers to whom the business owes money. These may also be referred to as supplier or vendor payables. This report provides valuable information about how much you owe to your Suppliers and can provide insights as to when you should make payments, which can help with cash flow analysis. Accounts Payable are a Current Liability on the Balance Sheet.

Assets

Anything that your business owns or from which it expects to derive a future benefit is referred to as an asset. For example, the money in your bank or investment accounts are assets. The equipment or machinery that is used to run your business, and the amounts that customers owe you (Accounts Receivable) are also assets. Assets are of three main types:

Current assets are available to you within the next year without restriction, such as cash in the bank or Inventory.

Long term assets are restricted and are not readily available in the short term, such as an investment in another company, which usually cannot be sold immediately.

Property, plant, and equipment represents tangible items such as computers, furniture, machinery etc.

Balance Sheet

Refer to the section on Financial Statements.

Bill

When an individual or entity provides you with a product or service, they give you a document that provides details of the product or service and the amount payable. This is referred to as a bill.

Budget or Forecast

When you want to predict your business performance over a specific period in the future, you will need to prepare a budget or a forecast. This is a very useful exercise for many business owners, even if only for their own purposes, as it allows them to see how they expect their businesses to perform. This can then be compared to their actual results and analysed to determine the reasons for the difference. You can use the Profit and Loss Statement as a template to predict your sales and Expenses for the coming year or for several years into the future. For more granularity, you can create a monthly budget. Many business owners find it difficult to make Estimates particularly when they are just starting their businesses, but as you accumulate history for your business, the process becomes simpler.

Chart of Accounts (COA)

A Chart of Accounts is the structural framework by which you summarize all the data that is entered into your accounting system. Each transaction that is entered is assigned to an account that is then condensed on an accounting report, such as the Profit and Loss Statement.

Cost of Goods Sold (COGS)

The direct costs of selling your product and sometimes services (if you have significant direct costs) are collectively referred to as Cost of Goods Sold. This will include costs to purchase the raw materials or items that you sell, packaging of your product, shipping and duties, labels etc. COGS also includes the cost of the labour to produce the goods.

Customer

An individual or business that buys your products or services. Can also be referred to as a client, particularly for service-based businesses.

Equity

When you deduct liabilities from your assets, the result is known as equity (or negative equity if your liabilities exceed your assets). Equity usually comprises the total contributions by the owner AND the accumulation of profits and losses since the inception of the company less any amounts withdrawn by the shareholders or owners in the form of direct withdrawals or dividends.

Expense

Costs that you incur that relate to your business and which are not included in Cost of Goods Sold are referred to as expenses. These are usually indirect costs or overhead costs that must be incurred to run your business. For accounting and tax purposes, expenses are categorized by type of expense which you set up via your Chart of Accounts. Some of the more common expense categories include:

- Salaries

- Rent
- Advertising and/or Marketing
- Office expenses
- Dues and subscriptions
- Travel
- Utilities
- Accounting and legal fees

Determining which expense categories are most relevant will depend on the specific requirements of the business. Having meaningful expense categories set up in your Chart of Accounts can provide a great deal of information and are especially useful for analysis.

Financial Statements

Please refer to the section on financial statements.

Property, Plant, and Equipment (Fixed Assets) and Depreciation

Items that are purchased for the business, that will likely last for at least one year and possibly much longer, are referred to as Fixed Assets. These include machinery, equipment, computers, furniture, and improvements. This also includes intangible items that provide long term benefits such as a customer list or a brand name or a special software/app that are usually costly to create and will last for several years.

Accounting recognizes that when you purchase a fixed asset, it will not hold on to its value forever. Rather, the value of most assets diminishes with the passage of time. This reduction in value in accounting terms is known as Depreciation (also known as capital cost allowance for tax purposes). There are several methods of depreciation which can be used to capture the loss most accurately in the value of the asset.

Gross Margin (GM)

The difference between your total sales and Cost of Goods Sold is referred to as the Gross Margin. This is also often expressed as a percentage by dividing the gross margin dollar amount by the total sales. The gross margin gives you insights into the direct costs of selling your product and can be used as a comparison to other businesses in your industry and various other types of financial analysis including determination of your breakeven point.

Inventory

If you sell goods, you usually have items that you have on hand but have not yet sold. Inventory includes items that have either been purchased, but not yet assembled and/or items that are fully assembled and ready to be sold. Inventory is a current asset on your Balance Sheet.

Invoice

An invoice is a document, presented to a customer by you, that indicates the details about a service for which the customer then owes you payment at a specified date. Invoices can have a variety of details and most commonly include the date, invoice number (which is often sequential), product or service being sold, details about the product or service, quantity, price per unit, amount, sales tax if applicable, and the total including sales tax.

Liability

When your business owes money such as a loan to a bank or shareholder, or to Suppliers for purchase of goods or services, it is referred to as a liability. Like assets, these are also classified as current for amounts that are due within the next year or long term for amounts that are only due after one year or more. An amount due to a supplier or taxes payable to the government are usually current, while a bank loan that has a fixed term exceeding one year is long term.

Profit and Loss Statement (P&L)

Please refer to the section on financial statements.

Retained Earnings (RE)/Owners' Equity

The accumulation of profits and losses, minus any dividends or distributions to shareholders, is referred to as retained earnings, which is a term that only applies to corporations. A sole proprietorship would simply reflect the accumulation of earnings as owner's equity on the Balance Sheet.

Sale

Anytime you sell a product or service or earn income for business purposes from another party e.g., a customer or client, it is referred to as a sale. From an accounting perspective, this is referred to as sales or revenues. There are conventional sales such as selling your cupcakes or web design services. Less conventional sales would include ad revenues from Google on your website or YouTube account, affiliate or referral commissions, or payments from a service such as Patreon or a Kickstarter/GoFundMe campaign. This also includes payments received in kind i.e., payments which are not received in the form of cash but a product or a free trip or subscription for which you would have to determine the fair market value and reflect them as sales.

Share Capital

The amount of money invested by the shareholder(s) of a corporation is referred to as share capital and is represented by common or preferred shares. This is included in the equity section of the balance sheet. Share capital represents an investment in a corporation whereas a shareholder loan (see below) is a debt, similar to a loan from a bank.

Shareholder/Owner Loan

The term shareholder applies specifically to corporations (as structurally you can only own shares in a corporation) while the equivalent term for a sole proprietorship would simply be owner. Often shareholders will lend or borrow money from their businesses. If they lend money to a corporation, it means that the corporation must pay them back. This is referred to as a shareholder loan payable. Conversely, amounts borrowed by the shareholder from the corporation are referred to as shareholder loans receivable since the money is owed to the corporation. Shareholder loans may be treated similarly to a third-party loan where interest is charged and/or there are specific payment terms. It should be noted that shareholder loans that are receivable by a corporation (i.e., when a shareholder borrows money from a corporation) have tax consequences if not repaid within a specific period of time. Please also refer to the chapter on borrowing money from the corporation.

> ➤ *Shareholder Loan and Share Capital are not the same things.*

Statement of Cash Flows

Please refer to the section on financial statements.

Supplier

An individual or business from whom you purchase products or services. Also referred to as a vendor.

SHOULD YOU DO YOUR OWN SMALL BUSINESS ACCOUNTING?

When starting your business, it is easy to be overwhelmed by the number of tasks you have to learn, one of which is accounting. While many business owners can cobble together a sense of their financial situation through (as a former boss used to say) "back of the envelope" calculations and reviewing their bank balances, there is still a need for an accounting system that can validate your calculations and provide you with data to ensure that your business is going in the right direction.

Setting up an accounting system can, however, be intimidating for many business owners. Accounting can be technical and requires an understanding of certain terminology to be most effective. Prior to technology, business owners would either have to outsource their accounting or hire personnel to take care of various entries and ledgers and consolidations. These days, however, there is a number of software and apps that can significantly simplify the process and allow any business owner that has a genuine interest in understanding their own data to do the accounting themselves. Answering the following questions can help you determine whether it makes sense to do it yourself:

1. **Are you a new(ish) business?**

   Probably the best time to set up your own accounting is when you are a startup or new(ish) business owner. This is because you likely don't have that many transactions and you might have some time on your hands while building up your business. Additionally, your requirements are much simpler in the early stages than when your business starts to become more established and consequently more complicated.

2.   **How many transactions do you have a month?**

If you expect your corporation to only have a small number of transactions, it makes sense to do your own accounting as these can be fairly easy to track with the right accounting software.

3.   **Do you prepare your own invoices for your clients?**

If you send invoices to customers/clients yourself, then setting up an accounting system right from the outset makes a lot of sense as this is a significant part of the work. All accounting software has the functionality to create and send invoices (many of them also have time tracking). With most software, you can email invoices to your customers from within the software and some even allow you to collect customer payments by clicking a link on the invoice. Payments collected directly are then posted and reconciled automatically, saving time.

4.   **Do you want real time data?**

For some businesses, having access to real time data can significantly benefit their operations. For example, if you sell handbags, you might need to track exactly what you have in stock at any given time and ideally you can depend on an accounting system to give you this information. If your operations are still relatively small, and you are already entering your own invoices, it is fairly easy to enter the other transactions to ensure you are up to date.

5.   **Do you need to** assess your cash flow **regularly?**

Some businesses need to know exactly where they stand with respect to their cash flow at any given time. Review of your bank balance gives you a sense of this; however, it does not tell you how much you owe to vendors or how much you are owed from customers. Additionally, you might have loans or interest payments that are coming due, or you might have other purchasing commitments that have to be met. If this is the case, you might want to consider doing your own accounting until your business is big enough to outsource or hire a bookkeeper.

6. **Are you comfortable with technology?**

   Having some experience with general purpose software and/or cloud-based apps is an important consideration when evaluating whether you should do your own accounting. If you haven't used technology much, the learning curve for a new accounting software will be steeper and as such will require a bigger time commitment.

7. **Do you like numbers, especially as they pertain to your business?**

   Do you have a sense of excitement when you see how your business is doing? Do you enjoy seeing how all the numbers come together and looking at your profit and loss? When you see your numbers, are you interested in deeper analysis, customer behaviour, what products or services are most popular, etc.? If so, doing your own accounting helps you be closer to your numbers, as you have a better understanding of the flow from original transaction to the final report, e.g., when you enter an invoice, it shows up a sale on your profit and loss report.

8. **Do you have an accountant or an accounting resource that is accessible for questions?**

   Since most business owners are not accountants, there are some technical transactions and treatments that can be difficult to wrap your head around. The day-to-day of entering your transactions can be fairly straightforward, but it helps to have a resource to whom you can turn when you are not sure how to do something, as this can help with you avoid mistakes that many small businesses make that can take some time to undo or, worse, result in incorrect reporting and potential penalties.

9. **Are you comfortable doing your own tax reporting?**

    Businesses have various tax obligations that are discussed in the tax section of this book. Some of the tax reporting is fairly easy and can be done by the business owner with a little bit of guidance. However, as your corporation grows in size, these obligations can become increasingly complex. As such it might make sense to do your own accounting while outsourcing your tax obligations to an accountant.

Cloud-based accounting software has significantly reduced the amount of time and knowledge required to do your own accounting. There are also numerous online courses and trainings available to help business owners navigate their accounting, making something that used to be quite inaccessible much easier to navigate.

WHAT ARE YOUR OPTIONS FOR DOING YOUR ACCOUNTING?

Use a Spreadsheet

I generally don't recommend using spreadsheet when you have a corporation. This is because the reporting requirements for a corporation, as explained in previous sections, are more onerous for tax purposes. There are numerous other reasons to use accounting software which are explained below.

Use Accounting Software

The accounting requirements for a corporation are more onerous than with an unincorporated entity. With a sole proprietorship, you usually only need a Profit and Loss Statement (P&L) for tax purposes. With a corporation, in addition to the P&L, you also at minimum require a Balance Sheet.

An accounting system can be an extremely powerful tool for business owners. When structured with the specific needs of the business in mind, it has the power (through the magic of debits and credits) to convert data into a format that tells an interactive, completely personalized story about your business.

There are several reasons why accounting software is the best tool for managing your corporation's financial data:

How Much Money Do You Have in Your Bank Account?

Many business owners, in the absence of an accounting system, will just look at their bank balance to determine their available funds. This method has limitations in that it does not reflect transactions that have not yet been processed including outstanding cheques, deposits, pre-authorized payments, etc. This can result in unnecessary overdraft charges and payments being declined, which can be detrimental to your credit rating (along with the headaches of dealing with the payee, bank, etc.). Ensuring that all banking transactions are properly recorded in your accounting system allows for a thorough review, which helps to prevent against unauthorized and erroneous transactions. Accounting software also facilitates the bank reconciliation process, which allows you to verify that every bank transaction has been entered thereby ensuring the completeness of your records. Once you have set up a system to track all banking transactions, the amount of available funds in your accounts is readily accessible and appropriate decisions can be made.

How Much Do Your Customers Owe You?

Knowing your exact Accounts Receivable balance, i.e., what customers owe you at any given time, is an essential component of a good accounting system. Even if you only have a handful of customers who pay on credit, it is important to know the amount of funds to expect once they paid and to ensure that the payments received match the amounts invoiced. Your business may be generating significant revenue, but if you have not yet been paid it can have an adverse, unexpected effect on short term cash flow. Also, following up on delinquent customer receivables on a regular basis is far more effective when done earlier, rather than months after the goods or services have been provided and can help reduce bad debts. Finally, accounting software can help you generate statements that can easily be sent to customers on a regular basis, saving time and reducing errors.

How Much Do You Owe Your Suppliers?

Tracking your bills can you help you optimize your cash flow and avoid unpleasant surprises. Ensuring that you only pay bills when they are due can free up your funds for other purposes. It also allows you to save money by taking advantage of discounts that are sometimes offered for early payment. Additionally, you can build a history of amounts paid to suppliers, which can be helpful when renegotiating terms, preparing annual budgets, or looking for new suppliers.

How Much Did You Sell?

An understanding of your sales is essential to know on an absolute basis and when comparing to a benchmark like your breakeven point and what you had forecasted. Your accounting software will allow you to structure your accounts so that you can track sales by different groupings including sales by category, item, type, or geographic region. This in turn can help you focus your sales efforts on products or regions that are more profitable.

What Were Your Total Expenses?

Any accounting system will allow you to track your individual expenses so that you can quickly identify how much you are spending, by different categories, e.g., labour, rent, supplies, raw materials, etc. Tracking your expenses on a spreadsheet, does not allow you to review history and comparatives. Once you have entered your expense data, you can analyze it by categories (in a Profit and Loss Statement) or review expenditures by suppliers or types of items purchased. By creating and modifying your chart of accounts, it is up to you decide how detailed you want this listing.

> ❖ *For example, if you are a manufacturer of pickles, you might want a separate account for cucumbers to assess the costs, which might give you some leverage with suppliers in the future if you can demonstrate how much you actually spent.*

What Were Your Gross Margins?

A key metric for businesses that sell products is referred to as gross profit or gross margin, which is calculated by deducting direct costs (cost of goods sold) from sales. As a percentage of sales, this can communicate whether you conform to industry standards, how to implement greater economies of scale, and how much you have left over to spend on overhead.

How Profitable Is Your Business?

Understanding the profitability of your business is perhaps the most important number for many business owners, both on an absolute basis and relative to prior periods or benchmarks. It also contributes to many business decisions including cash flow forecasts, how much to pay employees in bonuses, pricing of your goods or services.

How Much Did You Contribute to The Business?

Many business owners contribute to their businesses, particularly in the early stages, either by purchasing shares/equity, or through loans that will be repaid back once the business is generating enough cash flow. Your accounting system will help you keep track of how much you have contributed to the business either by accumulating it in a shareholder loan or equity account. You can also calculate your return on equity dividing the net profit of the business by the amount of equity that was contributed. The return on your equity (or investment) helps you to determine whether investing in a business results in a higher return than simply investing in another investment such as real estate or the stock market.

How Much Cash Flow Did You Generate?

Knowing your cash flow position is essential to the survival of any business. A cash flow deficit that cannot be covered can mean the end of an otherwise successful enterprise. There are businesses that have a profit but may have a negative cash flow due to high accounts receivable (amounts owing by customers), investments in equipment, too much inventory, etc. Most accounting software will let you know exactly how much cash you have on hand at the present and provide budgeting tools so you can estimate your future position.

How Much Inventory Do You Have on Hand?

For companies that manufacture and sell products, selecting an accounting software that can handle inventory such as item classification amount of inventory on hand, price levels etc. can have a huge impact on how your service your customers' needs, and allow you to control the amount of inventory you have at any given time. There is a cost both to not having enough inventory and having too much inventory. You should be able to understand your inventory needs, seasonality, supplier lead times and any other relevant metrics.

How Much Debt Do You Have and What Are the Related Interest Costs?

The total amount of debt owing should be tracked regularly to ensure that payments are made on time, interest expense is accurately calculated and debt to equity and other ratios are monitored to ensure compliance with debt covenants. Banks can be very strict where it comes to maintaining covenants and conditions on borrowing, so you don't want to be offside where it comes to fulfilling these requirements and having your line of credit or loans withdrawn.

How Much Do You Owe in Sales and Income Taxes?

Most accounting software have sales tax modules, specific to your country or region, that allow you to track exactly how much you owe (or are owed) at any given time. Since this is a significantly liability that can negatively impact cash flow, it is very important to know how much you owe and ensure you have the funds to pay it by the due date.

Business income taxes are not usually specifically tracked in accounting software but can be easily estimated periodically. You can also track instalment payments that are made towards taxes and set reminders as to when the payment is due.

How Can You Save Money?

A well-structured accounting system will provide you with enough info to identify areas where you can save money whether you simply spend less on certain items, renegotiate terms with a supplier, reduce bank charges or buy greater quantities, there are numerous opportunities to reduce costs. You also adjust your prices to increase profitability and review changes to your sales and expenses to determine the ideal balance.

Do You Require a History of Your Transactions?

One of the primary benefits of using accounting software is that it allows you to see a history of all your transactions. This is especially important when you have more than a few transactions a year. You can review transactions by customer to see what types of products they have purchased in the past and at what time of year. You can review supplier reports to determine if there have been price changes. You can see how a well a specific type of product has sold. You can review the number of hours you spend on a monthly or annual project for a customer. You can compare sales and expenses by various categories. There are numerous types of analysis which you can easily generate reports for (rather than combing through spreadsheets and compiling the data).

Do You Want to Simplify Your Sales Tax Filings?

Most accounting software allows you to set up sales taxes that are then easily assigned to invoices to customers and expenses. The total of these transactions populates a sales tax report that has all of the information that is required for the GST/HST filings. It simply needs to be transcribed on to the actual sales tax report, which can greatly simplify the process of filing your sales tax, improve accuracy, and produce a detailed report that can then be used in case of audit. Another benefit is that you can attach source documents to transactions, which can make an audit or internal review of transactions even easier.

Outsource to an Accountant

A third option for doing your accounting is to have an accountant take care of your books. While this makes sense if you don't want the hassle of doing your accounting yourself, the downside is that you don't have the visibility and control that you would if you were to do it yourself as discussed in the section above. The cost is also usually higher.

Even in this case, you may find it desirable to use accounting software to maintain a set of your own records. Your accountant would keep this software up to date.

HOW TO INVOICE YOUR CUSTOMERS/CLIENTS

After you have incorporated your business and registered for sales taxes, if applicable, you can go ahead and invoice your client and/or customer.

> ➢ *You cannot invoice a customer/client prior to the date of incorporation as technically the entity does not exist.*

How to Prepare an Invoice

Invoicing can be done in the following ways:

- Use word processing software or even a spreadsheet. A template can be set up that can then be saved as a PDF file and emailed or printed and mailed to your customers.

- Accounting software is recommended when you have more than a few invoices a month as it can result in significant efficiencies and allows you to review your history by customer, product, or service, etc. (reporting options are endless). You can set up one or several templates in accounting software, upload your logo, set up sales tax codes to apply automatically to specific customers, etc.

- Invoicing apps are particularly convenient when you are visiting clients, as with tradespeople or home-based services. These allow you to generate an invoice on the spot and also accept payment using a credit card processor. Several payment processors will also provide you with a handheld terminal that you can use to process payments as well.

- Handwritten receipts (although these are becoming less common since most people have a smartphone or technology at their disposal).

Information to Put on an Invoice:

An invoice can have some or all of the following fields:

- Name of customer
- Date of invoice
- Invoice number
- Address of customer
- Your company name and/or logo
- Your contact details
- Type of product/service being provided
- Rate and Quantity or Total Amount
- Description of products or services
- GST/HST number issued by CRA (usually ends with RT0001)
- GST/HST amount
- Total including sales taxes
  Payment details, e.g., wire transfer or e-transfer info

> ➢ *It is obligatory to include your GST/HST numbers on invoices or receipts to customers.*

Sales Tax and Invoicing

If you are registered for sales tax, it is mandatory to put your sales tax numbers on the invoice. If you are doing it using a spreadsheet, you can usually put them either under the customer contact info or in the main body of the invoice (or anywhere you like as long as they are visible on the invoice).

HST and GST rates are usually based on the location of the customer.

> ❖ *For example, if you are a Manitoba based company that provides web development services to customers in Ontario, you would charge them HST at the rate charged in Ontario, which is 13%. Similarly, if you were invoicing a customer in British Columbia, you would charge them GST only, which is 5%.*

There are several provinces that have Provincial Sales Tax (PST) in addition to GST. It is important to note that you are only required to charge GST or HST to customers in other provinces. Since PST is not part of the Federal GST/HST regime, it only applies if you have a presence or certain amount of sales in that province.

If your customer is outside of Canada, you are not required to charge GST/HST. However, you should make yourself aware of any international sales taxes that might apply in your situation.

> ➤ *Note: As with all matters relating to tax, the rules relating to sales tax can be much more complicated. The rules described above apply to typical and straightforward situations.*

WHAT TO LOOK FOR IN AN ACCOUNTANT?

Unlike accounting and tax for a sole proprietorship, which can be relatively simple for business owners to do on their own, corporations require a higher degree of expertise. Tax compliance for corporations is more rigorous and tax regulations are more complex. Consequently, I usually recommend identifying your needs and finding an accountant that can help meet them.

Below are some of the qualities that should be considered when looking for an accountant:

Responsiveness

Accountants who don't respond to their clients' emails and calls on a timely basis is perhaps the most frequent complaint I hear from unsatisfied business owners. One of the issues is that accountants, like lawyers, often charge their clients based on time, which is a bit more difficult for "quick questions". More and more accountants are however charging a fixed monthly or annual fee that includes a certain amount of interaction. Regardless, it is important to find an accountant who responds to your queries in a timely fashion.

Adding Value

The role of accountants has evolved over time. In addition to accounting and tax assistance, small business owners are looking for a professional to provide advice and guidance on various business issues. You should feel comfortable reaching out to your accountant on financial matters and while they may not always have the answers, they should be able to point you in the right direction.

Technical Competence

Your accountant, while not necessarily being a specialist, should have a strong understanding of accounting and tax matters especially as they pertain to small business corporations. Of course, accountants are not perfect and sometimes they make mistakes or omit something from a tax filing. In these cases, it is important they take responsibility, follow up, and resolve these issues quickly.

Rates

It is important that you and your accountant discuss billing rates and practices in advance so that there are no surprises. Clients often do not anticipate the amount of time it takes to complete certain tasks or research financial and tax matters, which is often the result of the accountant not setting the proper expectations.

Communications

Many small business owners have told me that their accountants are not very good at explaining financial concepts or tax requirements. While many of these concepts are somewhat technical, small business owner are usually able to grasp at least the gist as it so closely relates to their businesses. It is important that your accountant doesn't gloss over important information.

Choosing the right accountant doesn't have to be difficult. Ideally you want someone who is the right fit, and with whom you feel comfortable discussing the various financial aspects of your small business. They should be involved with more than just your annual tax filings and should feel like a partner to your business.

PART 3: Tax

WHAT ARE THE OBLIGATIONS FOR A TYPICAL CORPORATION?

Once you have incorporated your business, you will receive a variety of notices from CRA informing you of your tax obligations. Many of these notices contain business jargon that is not always easily comprehensible, especially to a new business owner. Unfortunately, simply ignoring these notices does not make your tax obligations go away. It is therefore prudent to understand exactly what your tax obligations are, which will help you to avoid interest, penalties, and unpleasant letters and visits from the government.

The following represents the tax filings and obligations for most small businesses:

Sales Tax Returns

If you are a Canadian small business that has more than $30,000 per year in revenues, and you are not considered to be Exempt or Zero-Rated, you are required to register for, and file periodic GST/HST. You can register for annual, quarterly, or monthly filings depending on the amount of your sales.

Payroll Filings:

If you have employees to whom you are paying salaries, you have two main obligations:

- Deductions at source returns, which represent the deductions taken on salaries/wages paid to employees. You are required calculate and remit the amount of deductions at source owing to government either monthly or quarterly. CRA will send you letters advising you of the required frequency.

- Annual T4 slips and summaries, which represent the total salaries paid along with information on deductions taken.

Other obligations might include annual workers compensation returns, which are provincially administered. This includes CNESST in Quebec.

Dividend Declarations

Shareholders of a corporation may also pay themselves dividends either in addition to or instead of a salary. The total dividend withdrawals during the year should be added up and declared as dividends. Even if you did not actually withdraw the funds, you can still declare a dividend for a specified amount. Once declared, a T5 form must be submitted to CRA indicating the amount of the non-eligible dividends and complete the other relevant information on the form.

Although the CRA and provincial revenue agencies are generally good at keeping businesses apprised of their filing obligations, notices are sometimes unclear or get lost in the mail. Ultimately, the onus is on the business owner to ensure that tax reports are filed on time and related amounts are paid. One of the best ways to keep on top of this is to register your business online with CRA.

Corporate Income Tax Returns

All incorporated businesses are required to file a corporate income tax return, which is also referred to as a T2, within six months of the year end of the corporation.

Annual Returns

Separate from the corporate tax returns, all incorporated businesses are required to renew their business registration. If your business is incorporated Federally, you are required to file the Annual Return on a yearly basis with Industry Canada. You will receive a notice from Industry Canada, either by mail or email, informing you that return must be filed, how to do it and the date by which it is due. Various provincial bodies also have their own filing requirements and forms, which can often be submitted as part of the corporate tax filing. If this is not done on a timely basis, it can result in delisting of your business.

WHAT IS SALES TAX AND SHOULD YOU REGISTER?

Sales tax in Canada is a mechanism by which the final consumer of goods or services, who is resident in Canada, is charged a tax for consumption of the goods or services provided. Although the tax is meant for the final consumer, which is almost always an individual, every business that is registered must charge every Canadian customer, regardless of whether they are a business or individual (subject to certain exceptions). If the customer is also a business that is registered, they can then claim back any sales taxes paid for expenses that relate to their businesses.

> ➢ *Only Canadian customers are charged sales tax. If your customer is based outside of Canada with no Canadian presence, you do not have to charge them sales tax. You might however have to charge them sales tax based on the jurisdiction in which they are located (such as European VAT, US sales tax (the rules for which are specific to each state), or Australian GST).*

In Canada, the Federal sales tax is referred to as Goods and Services Tax (GST) or Harmonized Sales Tax (HST), depending on the province in which you are located. Additionally, four provinces have their own provincial sales tax that is independent of the GST/HST. More details on provincial sales tax can be found in the appendices.

Once you have incorporated, you must consider whether you are required to register for the GST/HST. The simple answer is that if you anticipate that your annual gross revenues (total sales) are going to exceed $30,000 and your products and/or services do not qualify as Zero-Rated or Exempt, then you are required to register for GST/HST. Zero-Rated or Exempt businesses are those that provide products or services on which sales taxes do not apply and are explained below.

> ⚠ ***Taxi operator or commercial ride-sharing driver***
>
> *If you are a self-employed taxi driver or commercial ride-sharing driver (which refers to services such as Uber and Lyft), you must register for the GST/HST regardless of your revenues. This effectively means that you have to register on the day that you start operating your business.*

Should You Register Even If You Expect Less than $30,000 in Annual Sales?

Even if you do not meet the threshold of $30,000 (referred to as a "small supplier" by CRA) for mandatory registration or if you are providing Zero-Rated goods or services, it might still make sense to register. Consider the following:

Reasons to Register for GST/HST Even If Your Sales Are Less than $30,000

- The primary benefit of registering for sales tax is that it allows your business to claim back 100% of GST/HST that you have paid on business-related expenses. This is particularly helpful to start-ups and businesses that have high up-front costs such as computers and equipment as well as rent, office expenses, travel etc. Many such businesses have little to no sales in the first few months of starting their businesses and the recovery of sales taxes can help reduce costs significantly.

- Not being registered for sales tax can communicate to your clients that you are small and by extension might imply a lack of professionalism and/or experience.

- Since customers/clients expect to pay sales taxes anyway, it is rarely a deal breaker. Also, if your customers are primarily businesses, it has no real impact on their bottom line as they are able to claim back their businesses related sales taxes as well.

- If you don't register when starting your business, and your sales reach the $30,000 threshold, you will have to start charging sales tax, which will result in a sudden price increase of 5% to 15% depending on the province in which the customer is located. This is an issue especially for businesses that sell to individuals as they cannot claim back the sales tax that they pay.

> ➢ *If you are registered for sales taxes, you are required to charge them even if your sales are less than $30,000.*

Reasons to not Register for GST/HST If Your Sales Are Less than $30,000

- For those that have started a side or hobby business such as selling goods on eBay or providing web development services in their spare time and who don't expect their businesses to reach $30,000 in sales, at least for the foreseeable future, you might not want to take on the administrative burden of registering for sales tax.

- If you are primarily providing goods or services to individuals or businesses who are not themselves registered for GST/HST, it may be a competitive advantage if you do not register for and thus do not charge GST/HST, since your price will be lower compared to businesses that are registered for sales tax. Remember that, if your sales exceed $30,000, you will have to register.

- If you want to reduce your administrative burden and not have to worry about tracking sales taxes and potentially paying penalties and interest for late filings.

- If you are still in the startup stage and not sure about the viability of your business idea, it might not make sense to register right away.

> *The determination of whether you have reached $30,000 in sales in based on a rolling four quarter period. Review your sales every quarter to determine if you have reached or exceeded $30,000 over the past four quarters. As soon as you do, you are no longer a small supplier at the end of the month following the quarter in which you exceed $30,000 and must register.*

What Does It Mean to Be Zero-Rated?

Products and services on which you are not required to charge GST/HST are referred to as Zero-Rated. Included in this category are prescription drugs, groceries, and exports outside of Canada, including services provided to American and international customers. Small business and self-employed individuals whose goods or services have been designated as Zero-Rated, can still register for GST/HST (see above) as they are allowed to claim the Input Tax Credits (i.e., sales taxes paid for supplies and expenses, also referred to as ITCs). For example, if you provide services to clients internationally (e.g., the United States), you are not required to charge GST/HST in most cases; however, you may still claim back any GST/HST paid on business expenses. This can be a substantial benefit for businesses and freelancers.

See links below to see list of Zero-Rated supplies:

- Canada Revenue Agency (CRA) Zero-Rated Supplies and Services

What Are Exempt Supplies and How Are They Different from Zero-Rated?

Exempt supplies are also not subject to GST/HST and include items such as residential rental units, most health, medical and dental services, and educational services. The difference between Zero-Rated and Exempt is that, with the former, your business may claim back sales taxes paid on expenses (ITCs) while with Exempt goods and services you may not claim sales taxes on expenses paid. If you do provide only Exempt services such as doctors and residential landlords, you would not register for GST/HST.

See link below to see a more comprehensive list of exempt supplies:

- CRA Exempt Supplies and Services

Deciding whether to register for GST/HST is a determination that should be made based both on the tax requirements as well as business considerations. If you do not decide to register right away, you can always do so in the future. However, keep in mind that you might lose the ability to claim tax paid on expenses previous to your registration date, which can add up, particularly for businesses that have high start-up costs.

SHOULD YOU OPT FOR THE QUICK METHOD OF REPORTING GST/HST?

If you expect to have annual sales not exceeding $400,000, it might make sense to select the Quick Method of reporting your GST/HST, which is essentially a simplified method of reporting sales taxes. While regular reporting of sales taxes requires that you calculate all amounts collected and paid on eligible expenses, the quick method (or simplified method as it is also referred to) requires the application of a single reduced rate to your sales while GST/HST paid on expenses is not deductible. The primary benefit of registering for the Quick Method is to save money on the GST/HST that you have to pay to CRA. The key details of the Quick Method and its suitability for your business are discussed below.

What Are the Eligibility Criteria to Use the Quick Method?

For GST/HST purposes, annual taxable sales must be less than $400,000.

There are exceptions to businesses that are permitted to use the Quick Method. The following types of business **cannot** use the Quick Method:

- Accountants/Auditors/Tax Consultants
- Financial Consultants
- Lawyers
- Municipalities, Colleges and Universities, and Charities

What Are the Rates Used for the Quick Method?

GST

If 40% or more of your sales are from goods that were purchased for resale (e.g., all objects or things that may be perceived by the senses and are movable at the time of supply: a vehicle, animals, furniture, etc.):

- GST Rate is 1.8%

If your cost of goods sold is less than 40% (effectively, you are a service-based business):

- GST rate is 3.6%

For GST, you are eligible for a 1% credit on your first $30,000 of sales when using the Quick Method.

HST

HST Quick Method Rates depend on the province.

> ➢ *Note: The Quick method does not affect the actual rate of GST that is charged to customers and clients, which is 5%.*

When to Use the Quick Method

Since the Quick Method is simpler than the regular method of reporting GST/HST, it can be a great way to fulfill your tax reporting obligations while simplifying your accounting system.

The Quick Method of remitting GST can result in a significant savings; however, this is largely dependent on how much GST you pay on purchases (also known as Input Tax Credits). For example, a service-based business that uses the quick method rate of 3.6% and has $50,000 in taxable sales and $5,000 in taxable purchases would save $660, which can add up over time.

Since the Quick Method implicitly reflects Input Tax Credits (sales taxes paid on expenses) by reducing the rate that has to be remitted to CRA, no separate calculation for expenses is required (nor allowed). As such, taxes cannot be claimed on purchases/expenses except with respect to sales taxes paid on capital purchases like a car, computer, or real property, which are claimable. A capital item represents a purchase that has a useful life exceeding one year and usually exceeds $400.

However, a business that has higher costs in the beginning such as a startup might actually be paying more by using the Quick Method as their purchases exceed the threshold at which the Quick Method results in net savings. It is extremely important to make this determination before electing to use it. On the other hand, if you only have a small number of expenses, like many service-based businesses such as consultants, programmers, and contractors, it can make a lot of sense to use the Quick Method.

How to Register for the Quick Method

To start using the Quick Method for GST/HST anywhere in Canada (except Quebec), you must complete election form GST74 Election and Revocation of an Election to use the Quick Method of Accounting. The application can also be made using CRA's *My Business Account*.

The deadlines for the application for the Quick Method are as follows:

- For Quarterly or Monthly returns, it must be before the due date of the filing. For example, if you file quarterly and your due date is April 30th for the period from January 1st to March 31st, the election must be filed by April 30th.

- For Annual returns, it must be no later than the first day of the second quarter. This would be April 1st for all businesses with a year end of December 31st. For any other year end date that is not the calendar year, the due date for the election is three months + 1 day after the year end.

> ➢ *Note: Once the election has been approved, it can be revoked after waiting for a minimum of one year.*

WHAT YOU NEED TO KNOW ABOUT
REGISTERING FOR SALES TAX

If you are located anywhere in Canada (except Quebec), the administration of GST/HST is done by Revenue Canada. If you are located anywhere else in Canada and also have business in Quebec, you would register with CRA for GST/HST and then register separately for QST in Quebec (discussed in the appendix chapter on Quebec). If your business is located in Quebec, you would register for both GST/HST and QST with Revenue Quebec. Additionally, if you need to register for sales tax in British Columbia, Manitoba, or Saskatchewan, you would register for sales tax separately in each of those provinces.

> ➤ *The process for registering a sole proprietorship, partnership, or corporation for sales taxes is all essentially the same.*

> ⚠ *If you are changing your business from a sole proprietorship to a corporation, you MUST register a new business corporation and apply for new GST/HST numbers if applicable.*

How to Register for GST/HST

You may register for GST/HST in one of four ways:

- ONLINE: By accessing the CRA application.
- PHONE: By calling 1-800-959-5525.
- MAIL OR FAX: By mail or by fax by completing the RC1 form and supplying the information for the business accounts that you need.

- If you are using a service provider or lawyer to do your incorporation, you can ask them to register for sales tax at the same time.

What Type of Information Do You Need to Register?

The information required to register for GST/HST can be viewed on the RC1 Form, which as discussed above can either be completed and sent to CRA or will be required if you speak to them over the phone.

> ✓ The section of the form that is applicable to GST/HST registrants is Part B.

- The effective date of the GST/HST registration can be up to 30 days prior to the actual date of registration. However, if you did not collect sales tax from customers in this period, you cannot claim tax paid on expenses prior to this date. If you do want to register an effective date that exceeds 30 days prior to the registration date, you need to provide some additional documentation which is detailed in the section.

> ⚠ Your effective date of registration for sales tax CANNOT be before your date of incorporation.

- Total <u>annual</u> revenue from taxable sales and worldwide sales in Canada. This includes both sales on which GST/HST applies as well as Zero Rated sales, as discussed above. You may forecast an estimate.

- The fiscal year end should be the same as the year end that you selected for the corporation. The reporting period that is assigned to you is based on your expected annual sales volume:

- If your sales are under $1,500,000, you can choose an annual reporting period. You can also choose a quarterly or monthly reporting period.
- If your sales are between $1,500,000 and $6,000,000 you can choose a quarterly or monthly reporting period. You can however report annually.
- If your sales exceed $6,000,000, you must choose a monthly reporting period.

What Happens after You Register?

Once you have completed your registration, you will receive a GST/HST number. This is the same as your corporation business number except that the suffix is different and is usually followed by RT000?

> ✓ *The suffix on the top right of any notice received from the government helps you determine what file it relates to:*
> - **RT0001** refers to GST/HST
> - **RP0001** refers to Payroll
> - **RC0001** refers to Corporation Income Tax

Upon receiving the GST/HST number, you would update your invoice template to reflect the GST/HST number. Most accounting software will have a section where you can automatically input this information. If you are using a spreadsheet or document to create invoices, you can simply put it in the section with your business information or in the body of the invoice.

The GST/HST that you charge your customers is usually dependent on the province in which they are located. For example, if your business is in Alberta and you invoice a customer in Ontario, you would charge them 13% since that is the HST rate for Ontario, where they are located.

> ⚠ *Every province has either GST or HST. Some provinces*
> *also have a provincial sales tax, which is independent*
> *from GST/HST and must be registered for separately. See*
> *our section in the appendix.*

GST/HST Filing Obligations

After you have registered, you will usually receive a form in the mail depending on whether you registered for an annual, quarterly, or monthly filing. You must complete this form and submit it to CRA, along with the net of GST/HST collected from customers minus the GST/HST claimed on expenses, within the deadlines indicated on the form. Alternatively, the form can be filed online directly through CRA *My Business Account* or directly through the online business tax filing service offered by most banks.

How to Pay GST/HST Using Online Banking

All businesses, including sole proprietorships, partnerships, and corporations, that have a separate business bank account with a CRA-approved bank can make payments through the government tax payment and filing service. Signing up for this service can usually be done online: When you log-in to your business portal, the service can usually be found in the ***Bill Payments/Pay Bills*** section. Once you have agreed to the terms and completed the registration, you are ready to pay businesses taxes online. Each type of payment is represented by a different form that has to be "added" before payment can be made.

Below are a list of forms and their descriptions:

Federal Forms

GST/HST Return and Payment -- GST34 -- (GST34)

When you want to complete the entire GST/HST return online, this is the form to select. You are required to enter the period to which the return applies, whether quarterly, monthly, or annual. The due date is the date the return is due. Note that the filing should always be done at least one day prior to the due date as it usually takes one day to process. The due date reflected on the return can also be an earlier date (this will not make a difference to the due date that CRA have on file).

- Line 101 is total sales for the period being reported on.
- Line 105 is the GST/HST tax collected on the sales from line 101.
- Line 108 is the GST/HST tax paid on purchases.
- Line 110 allows you to enter instalments paid, if any during the year.

GST/HST Balance Due -- GST-B -- (RC177)

This is the form to use when you have received a Notice of Assessment for GST/HST and need to pay the amount due. This can be for interest and penalties or relate to a form that was filed but payment has not yet been made.

GST/HST Payment Only -- GST-P -- (GST-P)

This form can be used to make instalments for those who have annual filing periods, but whose GST/HST exceeds $3,000 and are therefore required to make quarterly instalments.

What Are the GST/HST Rates in each Province?

The GST/HST rates in each province are reflected in the table below:

Province	GST/HST Rate	PST
Alberta	GST 5%	None
British Columbia	GST 5%	7%
Manitoba	GST 5%	7%
New Brunswick	HST 15%	NA
Newfoundland and Labrador	HST 15%	NA
Northwest Territories	GST 5%	None
Nova Scotia	HST 15%	NA
Nunavut	GST 5%	None
Ontario	HST 13%	NA
Prince Edward Island	HST 15%	NA
Quebec	GST 5%	9.975%
Saskatchewan	GST 5%	6%
Yukon	GST 5%	None

What Are the Penalties for Late Filing Your GST/HST Returns?

The penalty for not filing the GST/HST return on time is 1% of the amount due + 25% of the amount due multiplied by the number of months is overdue, up to a maximum of 12 months.

❖ *Example:*

Balance Due		5,000.00
Number of months Overdue		2.00
Penalty Calculation		
1% of amount due	1%	50.00
25% of 1% of amount due	25%	12.50
Total Penalty		**75.00**

HOW TO PAY YOURSELF FROM A CORPORATION: SALARY VS DIVIDEND

While incorporation has many benefits for small business owners, it does introduce additional complexities that are not faced by unincorporated businesses (sole proprietorships, partnerships). While unincorporated business owners are simply taxed on their net business income, incorporated business must have a formalized structure through which to pay the owner; this usually takes the form of either salary or dividends or a combination of both. Either type of remuneration has tax and other financial implications that need to be considered before deciding which to use.

- Salaries are considered to be **active income** since they are paid to employees, while dividends are **passive income** that are paid to shareholders. Since RRSP contribution room is calculated on active (earned) income, if your only source of income is dividends, you will not be able to build RRSP contribution room nor benefit from the tax benefits. Similarly, childcare expense deductions are based on active income.

- Salaries are paid from pre-tax income, which means that they are tax deductible from the profits of your corporation. Dividends, however, are paid from after-tax earnings and are not tax deductible. To compensate for the additional taxes paid on a corporate level, CRA require the dividends to be "grossed up" (i.e., increased by a specific rate that approximates the amount of corporate taxes that would have been paid on the amount of the dividends). A tax credit is then available that is applied to the grossed-up amount, which results in lower income taxes payable on dividends declared on your personal tax return. The revenue agencies are interested in "integration" whereby the net taxes paid on salaries or dividends are approximately the same when you take both corporate and personal taxes into account. However, since it is impossible to achieve perfect integration, this is not always the case, which can create efficiencies and/or inefficiencies for the taxpayer, depending on the specific case.

- Salaries require additional administration in that you have to calculate, file, and pay your Deductions at Source on a monthly or quarterly basis. Late payments result in penalties and interest. At the end of the year, you have to file T4s along with related summaries. Dividend payments only require annual preparation of T5s (and RL3s in Quebec). No payment is due at the time of filing the T5, though quarterly instalments might be required if you consistently pay yourself through dividends and owe taxes at the end of the year.

- Salaries, within reasonable limits, can be used to reduce taxable business income down to the small business limit, which enjoys a lower tax rate. Care must be taken that the salaries paid are reasonable or they might be disallowed. Since dividends are paid from after tax income, they have no impact on profit.

- Canada Pension Plan (CPP) and Quebec Pension Plan (QPP) contributions are not payable on dividends. This can result in savings exceeding $6,000 for both employee and employer portions. The downside is that you will not be entitled to CPP/QPP benefits upon retirement. For 2021, the maximum monthly amount you could receive as a new recipient starting the pension at age 65 is about $1,200. Your monthly amount will depend on how much you have contributed to the plan and therefore if you are taking dividends and not contributing to CPP or QPP then you should have a solid retirement plan in place.

> ➤ *You can get an estimate of your monthly CPP retirement pension payments by logging into your My Service Canada Account.*

- When applying for the Scientific Research and Experimental Development (SRED) credit, eligible salaries are a significant part of the calculation, whereas dividends do not qualify for the credit. If the business owner contributes to the SRED project being claimed, it may make more sense to draw a salary to ensure a higher reimbursement.

- Salaries must be paid to employees of the company, while dividends must be paid to shareholders. Consequently, if you are not a shareholder then you cannot pay yourself dividends.

> ➤ *It should be noted that shareholders who own at least 40% of their corporations, whether they receive dividends or salaries, are not entitled to **Employment Insurance** (EI) and by the same token are not required to pay EI (if they take salaries) unless they specifically sign up for Employment Insurance for the self-employed.*

The choice of salary vs dividend depends on the specific circumstances of the business owner. It may be more beneficial to take out only the funds necessary to maintain your lifestyle while retaining any excess cash in your corporation, thereby deferring taxes. Alternatively, by taking out a salary, you may be able to maximize your RRSP and CPP contributions, which can reduce your tax liability.

DO YOU PLAN TO PAY YOURSELF A SALARY OR HIRE EMPLOYEES?

One of the benefits of being the owner of a corporation is that you can hire yourself as an employee and pay yourself a salary. Unlike a sole proprietor who is simply taxed on their business profits, the owner of a corporation can retain excess funds in the business thereby allowing them to defer tax.

You might also decide to hire one or more employees either at the beginning or as your business grow. The process of paying a shareholder of a corporation a salary or hiring employees is the same.

> ✓   *A corporate shareholder that owns more than 40% of a corporation is not entitled to claim employment insurance (since an owner cannot fire themselves) and is therefore exempt from paying employment insurance premiums. When setting up payroll for owners and family members of owners, it is important to remove any employment insurance premiums from the calculation of deductions.*

> ⚠   *When hiring a family member as an employee, you should ensure that you have a detailed job description and pay them a salary that is commensurate with what you would pay a non-related employee.*

HOW TO REGISTER FOR A FEDERAL PAYROLL ACCOUNT

The process for registering for a federal payroll account is similar to registering for GST/HST. Generally, upon incorporation you will be issued a Federal Business Number. If you do not have a one, you can also use the methods below to register for one.

- ONLINE: Register for a Business Number and payroll number online using this link. This will take you through an interview process where you submit the requested information. If you already have a Business Number, you would provide this and complete only the payroll section.

> Note: The online option is probably the fastest way to have your application processed.

- PHONE: Register by calling 1-800-959-5525.

- MAIL: Register by completing the Request for a Business Number form and mailing it to your tax center. This form also allows you to register for payroll at the same time, which is included in Part C. If you already have a Business Number, you would complete the payroll deductions form where you must include your Business Number, your business activity, and other information per the form above. Similar to registering online, the form requires you to indicate how many employees you intend to have over the next 12 months, how often you will pay them, and to answer a few other questions relating to the business itself. If you are not sure, you can use your best estimate. There is no penalty for changing the number of employees or estimated revenues etc.

> ✓ *You can register for a business number, GST/HST and payroll, or any combination thereof, at the same time using any of the methods described above.*

What are Your Options for Preparing Your Payroll?

Calculate It Manually

The CRA provides payroll calculators that allow you to calculate your deductions based on a specific salary or wage. They allow input of payroll period (weekly, biweekly, monthly etc.) and other amounts including union dues, taxable benefits, RRSP contributions etc.

If you do decide to do your salary/payroll calculations manually, you should track all salaries paid along with the specific deductions in a spreadsheet.

Another alternative is to use a free payroll calculator. Keep in mind that you will still have to maintain a detailed schedule of amounts paid.

The manual method of calculating your payroll and deductions is best for small business owners who want to save money and have extra time (or use a bookkeeper). The downside is that there is greater room for error that can result in costly penalties.

Use Accounting Software

If you want to keep your payroll in-house, there are several payroll software platforms that allow you do your own payroll, which is simpler and more accurate than doing it manually. In house software requires manual set up of employees and wage rates or salaries. Once set up, you enter the salaries or hours, and the software calculates the rest. Cheques can be printed directly from the software, and, in many cases, payroll software will also use direct deposit. It also compiles the data for remittance and year end reports; however, the business owner is responsible for ensuring that the reports and payments make it to the CRA by the deadlines.

Outsource to a Payroll Provider

There are numerous payroll providers in Canada to whom you can outsource your payroll. This is particularly useful when you don't have the time and/or are more comfortable having a more knowledgeable party take care of something that is somewhat technical in nature. The downside to outsourcing is that there is a cost associated with it.

Most payroll providers will take care of the monthly remittance of deductions at source to CRA and preparation of year end T4s and relevant summaries. It is important to be informed as to what the payroll provider will submit to ensure that all aspects of the payroll process are covered.

Hire an Accountant

The final solution for employers and business owners is to hire an accountant to take care of all your payroll needs. This removes the hassle of having to deal with it yourself, particularly if you do not have an in-house bookkeeper. Accountants will also ensure that all your filings and payments are kept up to date and ideally advise you about more complex payroll issues like taxable benefits etc. The downside is that accountants can be significantly more expensive than doing it manually, using software, or even outsourcing to a payroll provider. If you do already have an accountant that takes care of your other accounting and tax requirements, they will likely include payroll in their total package.

The choice of how to pay your employees depends on a variety of factors including how much control you want over the process, what you are willing to spend, and your growth expectations. It might make sense to start by doing it manually or using a free service in the beginning and transition over to a paid service as your business grows.

How Do You Pay Monthly Remittances (Deductions at Source) to Revenue Canada?

Once you have registered for a payroll account with CRA, you are ready to go ahead and make remittances. Note that employers must register for a payroll account before the "first remittance due date". The remittance due date is on the 15th of the month following the month in which you first pay your employee. Thus, if you issue paycheques to your employees in August, the payroll remittances (Deductions at Source filings) are due by September 15th unless you have received a notice allowing you to file quarterly or annually. This information is also usually available in CRA *My Business Account*.

Amounts to be deducted from employee paycheques and remitted to the CRA include Employment Insurance (EI), Canada Pension Plan (CPP), and Federal Income Taxes. There is also an employer contribution component of EI and CPP.

There are several options for setting up your payroll, paying employees, and calculating deductions at source. If you choose to submit the remittances to CRA yourself rather than outsourcing it to a third party, you have a few options:

- ONLINE (using Business Banking): Most Canadian banks (RBC, TD, CIBC, BMO, etc.) have a business banking section where you can set up and submit payroll remittances online, which is one of the simplest ways to file and pay the deductions at source. Once you have registered for the service, you would "add" the Federal DAS forms to the forms that are filed regularly. These are then to be completed based on your remittance frequency by entering the information for each field and replaces the paper form entirely. The remittance is then taken directly from the bank account.

⚠ *The filing date, when using online banking, is one business day before the stated due date, since the banks usually take one business day to process the payment.*

- ONLINE (using CRA *My Payment*): You may also complete the DAS (payroll remittance) form using *My Payment* where , similar to online banking, you would enter your account number, number of employees, and amount payable and then make payment using Interac, Visa, or Mastercard (debit only).

- MAIL: You can complete the form that you receive in the mail from CRA for monthly deductions at source and enclose a cheque with it. If you don't have the payroll form from CRA (which can happen in the first month after registration or if you misplace it), you can create a document that lists the payroll account number, number of employees, and the amount of the remittance and submit it. If paying by cheque, you should mail it a few days in advance to ensure it is received by the due date and thereby avoid penalties.

Other Options to Pay Deductions at Source

There are third party services that allow you to pay by credit card. Note that a fee is charged in addition to the amount due to

CRA. If you outsource your payroll to a third-party service such, they will take care of remittances on your behalf.

You can also make payment, along with a payment remittance from CRA, in person at a bank or the post office.

What Are the Penalties for Filing Payroll DAS Late?

It is very important to ensure that you pay your remittances on time. Failure to file the source deductions return and make payment will result penalties as follows:

- 3% if the amount is one to three days late;
- 5% if it is four or five days late;
- 7% if it is six or seven days late;
- 10% if it is more than seven days late or if no amount is remitted.

Interest will also be charged on late payments, and there are a variety of other penalties that may apply.

What Are Your Year End Payroll Obligations?

If you have employees, you are required to prepare and submit year end salary declarations to CRA, which are called T4s. If you do your own deductions at source calculations, you must keep track of the gross salaries and the various deductions. You can then download the physical forms from CRA and enter them manually (or by using the fillable PDF). If you use accounting software or a payroll service to calculate your salaries, they will generate a T4 for you and give you instructions on how to submit them.

HOW TO PAY YOURSELF DIVIDENDS

The owner of a corporation might decide to pay themselves a salary or dividends or a combination of both. This can change from year to year depending on several factors as discussed in the chapter on how to pay yourself.

If you decide to pay the shareholders of the corporation, there are several things you should know:

- Since dividend income must be reported as investment income on your personal tax return in the calendar year in which the dividends are paid or declared, it is important to ensure that you prepare the proper documentation for Revenue Canada (CRA). The dividend declaration that must be submitted for the calendar year is referred to as the T5 slip.

- As a shareholder of a small business corporation, you do not have to "declare" a dividend every time you borrow money from your corporation. Instead, the simplest way to track your dividends is to record any withdrawals that you take from the corporation in an account called "shareholder loan". Since, at the time of the withdrawal, you are borrowing money from your corporation, this is the appropriate accumulation account. It is important to note that CRA has significant restrictions with respect to borrowings by the shareholder from the corporation as discussed in this chapter.

- You can either prepare your own dividend declarations or ask your accountant to prepare them on your behalf. If you would like to prepare your own dividend declarations, you can refer to my comprehensive dividend guide that takes you through the process, step by step.

- The deadline for submitting the dividend declarations is February 28th of the year after the calendar year for which the dividends are declared.

❖ *If you declare dividends for 2021, the dividend declarations are due by February 28th, 2022.*

- Penalties for late filing of the T5 slip is $10 per day up to a maximum of $1,000, with a minimum penalty of $100.

CAN YOU BORROW MONEY FROM THE CORPORATION?

There are three primary ways in which you, as an owner and operator, can withdraw funds from your corporation. As discussed earlier, you can pay yourself a salary, or you can declare a dividend. Finally, you can borrow money from the corporation. When you borrow money from your own corporation, CRA has put into place strict rules as to when you have to repay the loan to ensure that the owner-manager does not avoid paying taxes indefinitely. When the owner-manager borrows money from the corporation, this is called a **shareholder loan** (money loaned **to** the corporation by the owner/operator is also a shareholder loan).

Shareholder Loan Balances

The basic rule for shareholders loans is that money owed **by** the owner/operator **to** the corporation must be paid in the fiscal year following the year in which the loan was taken.

> ❖ *For example, if your fiscal year end is December 31 and you borrow money any time in 2019, then it must be repaid before December 31, 2020.*
>
> ◆ *Failure to repay will result in the loan amounts being included in the shareholder's income in the year in which the loan was taken, which in this case would be 2019.*
>
> ◆ *CRA does not permit a series of loans and repayments, e.g., repaying an amount at the end of 2019 only to borrow it again in early 2020.*

The best way to clear out a shareholder loan balance is to pay a salary, bonus, or dividend (or simply repay it). Since this gives rise to taxable income and eliminates the shareholder loan for the previous year, it is not considered to be a series of loans and repayments.

Exceptions for Shareholder Loans for Specific Purposes

There are exceptions that allow shareholders to take out loans for longer periods:

- If a loan is made in the ordinary course of the corporation's business, e.g., they are a financial institution that makes loans as part of their business and as long as the terms of the loan are similar to an unrelated borrower.

- Purchase of shares in the corporation or a related corporation (this does not apply to unrelated corporations).

- Purchase of a motor vehicle for use in the employee's job.

- Trade debts, i.e., amounts sold by a corporation in the normal course of its business as long as it is on the same terms as other customers. Usually these are settled within 12 months.

- A final exception specifically includes the purchase of a dwelling (a house, condo, cottage, mobile home, and even a houseboat).

> ➤ It is important to note that this exception only applies if the same terms are available to all employees of a corporation, i.e., all employees may borrow funds from the business corporation to purchase a home. If you are the only shareholder of a corporation, it might be difficult to demonstrate that the same terms apply to all employees and there is a high chance that it will be disallowed.
> ➤ Keep in mind that, with respect to loans made to shareholders for the above purposes, a taxable benefit may arise for the shareholder if market rates of interest are not charged on the loans or one of the conditions is not met.

Accounting for Shareholder Loans

A shareholder loan account should be created as a current liability on the balance sheet. All withdrawals that are personal in nature should be allocated to this account, including cash withdrawals and purchases made through the corporation. This can be offset (reduced) by repayments by the shareholder in cash, or expenses paid personally by the shareholder that relate to the business, including gas, repairs, business portion of dues and subscriptions, travel expenses, home office expenses, etc. The total in the shareholder loan account at the year end previous to the current year end, once all transactions have been entered and adjustments reflected, should then be cleared out by declaration of a dividend or by payment of a bonus or a salary.

> ➤ If you are repaying the shareholder loan by issuing a bonus or from your salary, the net amount and not the gross should be sufficient to cover the shareholder loan balance.

> ❖ *For example, the portion of airline tickets that may have been purchased for a spouse accompanying you on a business trip or the personal portion of telephone expenses would be reflected in this account.*

The journal entry for a shareholder loan that is loaned by the corporation to the shareholder is as follows:

> **Debit:** Shareholder loan receivable or payable (it is best to have one shareholder loan account which is either a receivable depending on whether it is more often an asset or a liability).
>
> **Credit:** Cash/Bank

It is important for small business owners to understand that, although they may borrow funds from the corporation, they must repay these amounts by the end of the following fiscal year either via a direct repayment or via salaries or dividends. If not, the amount of the loan will be included in your income for the year in which the loan was taken, which can result in significant taxes payable as well as interest and penalties.

WHAT YOU SHOULD KNOW ABOUT CORPORATE TAX

There are essentially two types of tax returns for small businesses and the self employed. If you are an unincorporated sole proprietor or a partnership, you are required to fill out the statement of business activities (T2125) on your personal tax return (also referred to as the T1). If you are incorporated, then you are required to complete a corporate income tax return (referred to as a T2) that is specifically for the corporate entity. Although the accounting for unincorporated and incorporated entities is very similar, preparing the T2 is more complex and is often best outsourced to a qualified accountant. Regardless, it is always beneficial to have an understanding of some of the key components of a corporate tax return.

Corporate tax rates for small business are significantly lower than if you are unincorporated. The Federal rate, for businesses claiming the small business deduction, is 9% in 2021. Each province then levies additional taxes.

The table below presents the 3 types of rates that apply to corporations:

General is the rate at which income for corporations that do not qualify as small businesses are taxed.

Small business is the rate that applies to "active business income" (i.e., non investment income), that does not exceed $500,000. The corporations must also be Canadian Controlled Private Corporations (CCPCs).

Investment income refers to the corporation tax rate on investments, including rental properties and investment portfolios. CRA tries to discourage the creation of corporations simply to hold investments and therefore imposes a tax rate that is similar to the highest marginal tax rate for an individual. There are additional complexities including something called the Refundable Dividend Tax on Hand where a portion of the tax paid on investment income is refundable if dividends are paid out to the shareholder.

Corporate Tax Rates by Province

Province	General	Small Business	Investment Income
Alberta	23%	11%	46.7%
British Columbia	27%	11%	50.7%
Manitoba	27%	0%	50.7%
New Brunswick	29%	11.5%	52.7%
Newfoundland and Labrador	30%	12%	53.7%
Northwest Territories	26.5%	11%	50.2%
Nova Scotia	29%	11.5%	52.7%
Nunavut	27%	12%	50.7%
Ontario	26.5%	12.2%	50.2%
Prince Edward Island	31%	11%	54.7%
Quebec	26.5%	12.2% (20.5%)	50.2%
Saskatchewan	27%	0%	50.7%
Yukon	27%	0%	50.7%

> ➤ *The rates presented above include the federal general rate of 15% and small business rate of 9%.*

> ➤ It should be noted that, in Quebec, you must have employees that work a total of 5,000 hours per year to qualify for the Quebec small business tax rate. Otherwise, the corporate tax rate that pertains to Quebec is 11.5%.

> ➤ Permanent establishment: You might think that you can incorporate in a province with a lower tax rate such as Alberta and pay a lower rate of tax. This is a fallacy. Corporate tax is based on the concept of permanent establishment. This means that the corporate tax rate is based on where the primary decision makers of the corporation are located. Consequently, if you are the sole owner of your corporation and are based in Ontario, your corporate tax rate would be the Ontario corporate tax rate.

> ➤ If you have both small business income and investment income in a corporation, they will be taxed at the rates indicated above based on the source of the income.

Key Facts that You Should Know about Corporation Income Tax

Deadlines/Interest: Federal Corporate taxes payable are due three months after the year end for those corporations that qualify for the small business deduction. Interest will start to accumulate on any unpaid amounts after these deadlines (but no penalties until 6 months after the year end). This means that even if you do not file your tax return within these dates, you should estimate your taxes payable and remit these amounts to avoid interest.

GIFI: The method of accounting for revenues and expenses is generally the same as if you were unincorporated. The difference with a corporation tax return is that you are required to complete the General Index of Financial Information schedules on the T2 which is also referred to as the GIFI. This includes your Profit and Loss Statement, a Balance Sheet, and a Notes section, which is completed by the preparer of the tax return.

Business numbers: In order to file a corporate tax return, you will need to ensure that you have a business number. This is the same as your payroll/deductions at source or GST/HST number, with a suffix that ends in RC0001.

E-filing: Corporate tax returns can be e-filed directly through CRA *My Business Account* or by using approved tax software.

Instalments: Corporate tax instalments are usually based on the prior year's taxes payable and are usually due quarterly. Interest accumulates on unpaid amounts. If, however, you forecast that your taxable income will be lower in the current year vs the prior year, you can reduce your instalments payable accordingly.

Software: Most accountants use tax software to prepare income tax returns, who usually buy a package. Some of these software are also available on an individual basis to those business owners who want to prepare their own corporate tax returns.

WHAT TYPES OF EXPENSES ARE DEDUCTIBLE?

Generally, any expenses that are incurred to earn business income are considered to be deductible. Expenses are deducted from total revenues to calculate the net profit for your business. The amount of corporate income tax that you pay is based on the net profit of the corporation.

A corporation can deduct a variety of expenses. When deducting an expense, it is important to ensure that the expense is reasonable and actually relates to your business. Large amounts of expenses will raise a red flag with CRA, which can result in an audit where they might be disallowed. It can also result in interest and penalties and lead to being audited more frequently. This is especially applicable to "soft" expenses such as automobile, home office, and travel that often have a personal component.

Types of Deductible Business Expenses

- Direct costs of running your business including the raw materials, shipping, packaging, duties, wholesale purchases of goods for resale etc.
- Wages, Salaries, and Benefits paid to employees
- Amounts paid to subcontractors
- Rent, utilities, insurance, property taxes, and other office space costs
- Office supplies/services and equipment
- Information Technology Equipment/Services
- Software/Service Subscriptions
- Telephone expenses
- Conference expenses including travel
- Transportation costs

- Advertising expenses, which includes marketing, internet-based advertising, trade magazines, trade shows, website hosting and development etc.
- Professional dues such as those paid by doctors, lawyers, accountants etc.
- Accounting, legal, and business consulting fees
- Bank charges and interest on loans, including credit cards
- Credit card fees incurred on payments received from customers
- Meals with a business stakeholder such as a customer, supplier, accountant, subcontractor etc.
- Life insurance premiums (Only applicable where the beneficiary is the business)
- Depreciation on fixed assets (i.e., larger ticket items $400+) including Computer Hardware
- Automobile expenses for corporations can be claimed in several different ways including a simple per kilometre rate driven for business
- Home Office expenses are based on the percentage of your home that you use as your office as long as you don't have another office (with some exceptions)
- Uniforms and Clothing expenses are subject to certain restrictions which be reviewed before claiming them

Other Considerations for Business Expenses

- **Hobby Business:** Care should be taken to ensure that the business is not regarded as a hobby, otherwise tax deductions/expenses that exceed the income of the business will not be allowed.

- **Accrual Method:** Business are required to record their revenues and expenses based on the accrual method.

This means that both revenues and expenses are based on the date of the invoice/bill rather than when payment is received or made.

- **Keep All Receipts!** It is extremely important to keep all receipts, bills, invoices, cancelled cheques, and deposit slips. If you have any doubts, then keep it! Also, ensure that you retain all documents received from the government, including assessments and notices. A good practice with respect to business documentation is to scan it (or save electronic copies) in an accounting folder on your computer along with a backup. You may then dispose of any physical copies as long as you have a clear and legible electronic copy.

- **Business Loss Carry Forwards:** Losses incurred by a corporation may be carried back against income earned in the previous 3 years or carried forward 20 years. This allows you to recover tax that you have already paid or is payable.

> ❖ *For example, if you corporation's net loss for the fiscal year ended March 31, 2022 is $20,000 and the net profit for the year ended March 31, 2023 is $45,000 you will only pay corporate tax on $25,000 in 2023. This is because you were able to reduce the taxable income in 2023 by the loss incurred in 2022.*

Pre-Incorporation Expenses

Many potential business owners incur costs prior to incorporation that relate to their businesses. Technically, an entity that does not exist cannot have transactions and therefore would not be able to deduct pre-incorporation expenses. CRA, however, will normally accept the accounting for pre-incorporation transactions by a newly formed corporation if the following conditions are met:

- The facts clearly indicate that it is the intention of those persons who authorize the transactions in the situations described above that the business will be carried on by a corporation. This will usually be so where application for incorporation is made before or at the time the business is commenced or purchased.

- The period of time between the commencement or purchase date and the incorporation date is relatively short or, if not, the delay is not due to any action taken or not taken by the parties involved.

- There is no dispute between the persons authorizing the transactions and the newly formed corporation as to who will account for the transactions.

- The effect on the combined tax liabilities of the parties involved is negligible.

- The corporation adopts any written contract made in its name or on its behalf before it came into existence in respect of the pre-incorporation transactions it is accounting for.

(from Business Transactions Prior to Incorporation)

Essentially if you incur expenses that demonstrably relate to the new corporation within a reasonable period of time prior to incorporation, only one entity claims the expenses, and the impact of the transactions on the taxes payable is not significant, then you can reflect pre-incorporation expenses.

> ❖ *Examples of pre-incorporation expenses might include the costs of incorporation, advertising expenses, or purchases of materials that will be used in manufacturing your product.*

✓ *If you have equipment that you own personally and would like to transfer to the corporation, you would need to assess the fair market value, backed up by documentary evidence. For example, you can fairly easily assess the value of a computer of certain model and age from the internet, which you would then keep a record of. Once you have determined a reasonable value, you can simply transfer it to the corporation and either be reimbursed for the fair market value or add it the shareholder loan (the amount that the corporation owes the shareholder) and reimburse yourself at a later date.*

HOW TO SIGN UP FOR *MY BUSINESS ACCOUNT* WITH CRA

With all the data moving to the cloud these days and ubiquitous online access to banking, customer, and supplier portals, it makes sense that Revenue Canada (CRA) has followed suit. Considerable resources have been spent by the revenue agencies on developing their online portals and encouraging both individual taxpayers and businesses to move the majority of their tax-related interactions online. (Almost every accountant conference has an appearance by a CRA representative talking about the improvements to their online portal and imploring accountants to convince their clients to make the switch). The upfront investment has resulted in significant cost savings for CRA (postage costs alone have dropped dramatically) while improving accuracy and perhaps most importantly (for the government) increasing the effectiveness of tax collection efforts. CRA personnel have been able to move away from verifying calculations and manually reviewing tax returns to more value-added analysis, which has allowed them to identify tax miscreants with higher accuracy.

Benefits of Registering for *My Business Account* with CRA

For both the individual taxpayer and small business owner, there are numerous benefits to registering.

1. ***My Business Account*** for both CRA gives you access to:

    - Payroll deductions at source paid
    - T4 summaries and slips
    - GST/HST returns filed and payments made
    - Tax deadlines

- Taxes paid to date
- Instalment payments
- Correspondence from CRA
- Notices of assessment
- Statements of account

2. Ability to review all tax documents, including Notices of Assessment, in one place rather than having to save/scan them and inevitably lose them when needed most.

3. Being able to keep on top of tax obligations to avoid penalties, reduce interest charges, and running afoul of requests for information/audits due to missed or overlooked mail.

4. Submit documents relating to open queries/cases/authorizations online rather than faxing them in.

5. Consult statements of account to reconcile payments made to the various tax accounts. Often GST/HST refunds, instead of being paid out to the business, will get allocated to corporate or payroll taxes payable (or vice versa). Being able to review the statement can greatly facilitate the reconciliation process.

6. Consult year-end tax balances e.g. capital and non-capital loss carry forwards, refundable dividend tax on hand (RDTOH), and Capital Dividend account balances (once they are verified) are all available on the CRA site.

7. You can add your accountant as an authorized user using CRA **Represent a Client** allowing them to retrieve Notices of Assessment directly or reconcile accounts to payments made, communicate with CRA, etc.

8. GST returns can be filed online, which is simpler than mailing in the forms. It also provides details about payment options.

9. Year-end salary declarations including T4 slips can be filed online rather than having to complete these by hand, mail them in, and hope that they arrive on time.

How to Register for *My Business Account*

Online registration is also fairly straightforward. With CRA, identity verification can be provided by a banking partner, which can be seen on the registration page. You want to make sure that you have your Notices of Assessment handy, and then follow the instructions to register. CRA will usually send a security code either in the mail or it can also be retrieved by calling them. To register, click CRA *My Business Account*.

Registration itself may take some time; however, once completed, it can help you (and your accountant) to stay on top of your tax obligations.

WHAT ARE THE TAX FILING DEADLINES FOR A CORPORATION?

Tax deadlines for a corporation are not always on a specific date like they are for a sole proprietorship. Rather, some tax filings are due within a certain timeframe after the end of the period.

Corporate Income Tax Returns

Corporation income tax returns, or the T2 along with the relevant schedules, must be filed within six months after the fiscal year end of the corporation. If they are not filed within six months, penalties will apply based on the balance payable.

Interest starts to apply within 3 months after the year end for small business corporations.

Annual Returns

The deadline to file a Federal Annual Return is 60 days from the anniversary date of the incorporation. Provincial declarations vary by province.

Sales Tax Filings

For annual filers, the GST/HST returns are due within 3 months of the end of the GST/HST period, which is usually, but not always, the same as the fiscal year end.

For quarterly and monthly filers, the GST/HST return is due within one month of the end of the period.

> ⚠ *It is very important to verify your GST/HST reporting period, which can be done by either referring to the document that you receive from CRA confirming your reporting period or by going to the GST/HST section in CRA My Business Account.*

Payroll Filings

Deductions at source (DAS) remittances are most commonly due by the 15th of the month following the month in which salaries/wages were <u>paid</u>.

> ❖ *Salary/wage reporting is always based on the date paid rather than the date earned. If you pay your employees on December 5th for the month of November, the salary reporting would be for December, and the DAS remittances would only be due by January 15th.*

Some employers may submit and pay their DAS quarterly. If this is the case, CRA will notify you by letter.

> ➤ *Even if you have been selected as a quarterly remitter by CRA, you can still pay monthly without any consequences.*

Salary declarations, i.e., T4s, are based on the calendar year. The T4s must be submitted to CRA by the last day of February in the year after the calendar year in which the salaries were paid.

Dividend Declarations

Similar to salaries, the dividend declarations, i.e., T5s are also based on the calendar year end must be submitted to CRA by the last day of February in the year after the calendar year in which dividends are declared. The dividends don't necessarily have to be paid out but can simply be added to a shareholder loan payable.

Instalments

Depending on your corporate income and sales taxes payable, you might have to start paying quarterly or monthly instalments.

Quarterly income tax instalments are due if your prior year's corporate income tax payable exceeds $3,000. The due dates for quarterly corporate tax instalments are 3 months after the year end and every 3 months after that.

Quarterly sales tax instalments are also due if your GST/HST exceeds $3,000 and are due 4 months after the end of the reporting period with each subsequent instalment due 3 months after.

INVESTMENT STRATEGIES FOR INCORPORATED BUSINESS OWNERS

One of the benefits of having an incorporated small business is that, after paying yourself a salary or dividend, any excess funds can be invested directly through the corporation. Since small businesses often cannot predict how their business will perform from year to year, the ability to retain funds in the corporation allows for a cushion to smooth out fluctuations in earnings, which can then be paid out as a salary or dividend in lower performing years. By keeping the funds in the corporation, the business is able to defer tax, since the small business tax rate is usually lower than the personal tax rate. Some points to consider:

- Prior to leaving excess funds in the corporation, the business owner should take advantage of RRSP contribution room, particularly if you are in a higher tax bracket. Since RRSP contributions are tax deductible and the taxes on income earned are deferred until withdrawal (likely at retirement), this results in a higher after-tax income.

- Income earned on investments in a corporation is taxed at a higher rate (around 50% depending on the province).

- New (complicated) rules were put into place by the Federal government that taxes earnings in excess of $50,000 per year at a higher rate by reducing the small business deduction available to small business owners. If you are earning more than $50,000 per year on your investment income, I recommend getting professional accounting/investment advice.

- Investment vehicles for corporate investments are more restricted than personal investing and are generally more tax efficient.

If you have excess funds in your corporation that you do not plan to reinvest in the business (e.g., by purchasing equipment), or withdraw as renumeration, you can set up an investment portfolio. Below are some investment options for the owner-manager:

Large Banking Institutions

Perhaps the most popular small business corporate investments in Canada happen through business owners' banking institution, e.g., TD, RBC, CIBC, etc. Most have specialized investments and funds set up to assist the corporate owner. Note that fees are often higher with these institutions; however, it is certainly worth investigating.

Online Banks

There are numerous smaller banks that allow for corporate investment into savings accounts or GICs that offer higher interest rates, e.g., Oaken and Tangerine. There is often more paperwork required to set up a corporate account than a personal account as most banks will ask for documents relating to the corporation that usually must be mailed in. As such, this can be a somewhat time-consuming process. However, if the goal is to maintain excess funds in an interest-bearing account, it can be worth it to put in a little extra time up front to get a better return.

Robo Advisors

The popularity of robo advisors has skyrocketed in recent years due their simplicity and low fee structures. With a robo advisor, you provide details regarding your situation and risk tolerance, and they customize an investment portfolio for you that usually consists of exchange traded funds (ETFs). For example, if your risk levels are low, they will allocate a higher percentage of investment funds into bonds/money market vs equities. Examples of Canadian robo advisors include WealthSimple and Questrade.

Real Estate

As an alternative to investing in savings and investment funds, a corporation can also invest in real estate. It might make sense to purchase your office space instead of renting or perhaps invest in another property that provides rental income. The benefit of this is that although investment (passive) income will be taxed at approximately 50% in the corporation, the actual funds used for the down payment are taxed at lower corporate rates. Also, all related expenses including mortgage interest, property taxes, utilities, insurance, etc. are tax deductible. The corporation can either buy the property directly or set up a holding company and loan the funds to the new entity through an inter-corporate loan. (Note: any investments that involves setting up a holding company (holdco) should be discussed with a qualified professional as this might affect the active corporation's ability to claim the capital gains exemptions, among other tax implications). Real estate is a less liquid investment and as such should only be undertaken if funds are not required in the near term.

> ➤ *Although small business corporate investing is more restrictive than personal investing, there are still a number of investment options that allow you to earn higher returns than if you were to keep the funds in a checking or even a high interest savings account.*

APPENDICES

APPENDIX A: WHAT YOU NEED TO KNOW
ABOUT HAVING A CORPORATION IN QUEBEC

If you are planning to set up your corporation and operate in Quebec, there are some specific differences that every new corporation owner needs to know. In some cases, additional forms need to be filed while in others there is a completely separate procedure that replaces what is done in the rest of Canada. In this chapter I have enumerated the key differences.

Corporate Names in Quebec

In Quebec, it is obligatory to have a name for your corporation in French. There are a variety of strategies to meet this requirement.

Canada Corporations (and Corporations from Other Provinces)

In your corporation has both an English name and a French name at incorporation (e.g., *Colossal Computer Ltd. / Ordinateur Colossal Ltée.*) or a combined English and French name (e.g., *Ordinateur Colossal Computer Ltd.*), you would simply register the French version (or the combined English and French version) as the corporate name and the English name as a "version of the name in another language".

However, if you established a corporation Federally that has an English name only, you will have to register that as the name of your corporation (e.g., *Colossal Computer Ltd.*) and then register an additional name that is in French (e.g., *Ordinateur Colossal Computer*). This name will not contain a Legal Ending (e.g., Inc., Ltd.) as it is not a legal corporate name. Instead, this will be a "Doing Business As" (DBA) name.

Alternatively, you could amend your Articles of Incorporation to add an exact French version of the corporate name that would then feature a Legal Ending. There is a process and a fairly substantial fee involved, so if you are planning to establish a Canada corporation in Quebec, it's a good idea to start with both an English and a French name.

Quebec Corporations

For a Quebec corporation, the rules are straightforward: the government will not approve a corporate name that does not meet the French language requirement. Consequently, many entrepreneurs choose to establish a word name that contains an English Distinctive Element, a French Descriptive Element, and an English Legal Ending (e.g., *Colossal Ordinateur Inc.*), or a combined name (e.g., *Ordinateur Colossal Computer Inc.*).

Another strategy is to find a word in English that is the same in French that you can use as a Descriptive Element, like "chauffeur", "communication", or "techno".

As above, you may also register an English DBA once you have a French corporate name established.

How to Register Your Partnership or Corporation

When registering a corporation in Quebec, you have two choices:

- you can incorporate Federally and register the corporation in Quebec, or
- you can incorporate directly in Quebec.

Details about incorporating your business Federally can be found in the section on how to start your corporation.

For the specific procedures on how to incorporate or register your business in Quebec please refer to this page from the Registraire Des Entreprises.

What Happens After You Incorporate?

Once you incorporate your business, you will receive various documents from CRA, which includes your business number.

In addition, whether you incorporate Federally and register in Quebec or incorporate in Quebec, you will receive two additional numbers:

- Numéro d'Entreprise du Québec (NEQ) which is your business registration number
- Identification Number which is your tax identification number and will be used for all procedures relating to Quebec taxes.

> ✓ *Similar to tax documents received from CRA, the suffix on the top right of any notice received from the government helps you determine what file it relates to.*
>
> - TQ0001 refers to QST
> - RS0001 refers to Payroll
> - IC0001 refers to Corporation Income Tax

Registering for RQ *My Account for Business*: clicSÉQUR

The advantages for signing up for online access to your business files are the same as signing up for CRA *My Business Account*. In Quebec, this service is called clicSÉQUR (CS). Once you have signed up, you can get access to:

- GST/HST and QST filings, history and due dates
- Payroll filings, history and due dates

- Corporate tax filings, history and due dates
- Add users and change your contact details
- Register for GST/HST and QST and Payroll directly through the portal
- Statements of account
- Correspondence including notices of assessment

> ➢ *It is important to note that there are several different types of logins for Revenue Quebec businesses. When accessing the tax files, it is important to use the "my business account" link.*

How to Register for clicSÉQUR

Click on the my business account link.

Click on the "Access My Account" button and select "Inscrivez-vous!" and enter the information requested about your business.

> ⚠ *Note that you will be provided with a username and password. It is essential that you save or print the record which contains the username and password, otherwise you will have to call them which can be a tedious process.*

Once you have registered, Revenue Quebec will generally call you at the phone number provided during registration to verify your identity. You should also receive emails advising you of your registration.

> ➢ *Once you have registered your business in Quebec, you can also access the Registraire des Entreprises using the **clicSÉQUR** login and password at the clicSÉQUR Entreprises link to access details about your account, change addresses, and update your Annual Declaration.*

How to Register for Sales Tax in Quebec

The criteria for determining whether a business is required to register is the same as for GST/HST and discussed in this section. If you decide to register for sales tax in Quebec, then in addition to GST/HST, you must also register for QST.

> ➤ *Note: In Quebec both the GST/HST and the QST are administered by Revenu Québec. In the rest of Canada, GST/HST is administered by CRA.*

You can register for GST/HST and QST in one of four ways:

- ONLINE: By using the Register a New Business service (to register for sales taxes, payroll source deductions, and corporation income tax).

- ONLINE: By accessing My Account for Businesses, if you are already registered for clicSÉQUR with Revenu Québec (you can access the service in the Consumption Taxes section in My Account).

- PHONE: By calling Revenu Québec's client services.

- MAIL: By filing form LM-1-V: Application for Registration.

The information required is similar to CRA, except that the NEQ business identification number is also required.

After you register, you will receive a GST/HST number with a suffix ending in RT0001 and a QST number with a suffix ending in TQ0001.

You would then update your invoice template to include the GST/HST and QST numbers.

How to Pay Your GST/HST and QST

Since both GST and QST are administered by Revenu Québec, only one "Combined" form is required to pay both taxes. The following forms are available through the business tax filing services offered by most banks when you have a corporate bank account:

Combined GST/HST + QST Remittance -- G-QST -- (FPZ-500.IF)

This is similar to the "Federal - GST/HST Return and Payment -- GST34" explained above. The information required is the same plus the same line numbers for Quebec including 205, which is QST Collected and 208 which is QST Paid on Expenses.

Combined GST + QST Instalment -- TXIN -- (FPZ-558)

This form, similar to the Federal payment only form above, can be used to make instalments for those who have annual filing periods, but their GST/HST and QST each (individually) exceed $3,000 and are therefore required to make quarterly instalments.

> ➢ *Commercial ride-sharing driver*
>
> ⇨ *Uber will both automatically register you for GST and QST in Quebec and collect and remit the amounts due on your behalf. You simply have to prepare and submit the GST/HST and QST return at the end of the year.*

Revenue Quebec Payment Code

You can also file directly through your clicSÉQUR account. Once filed, a payment code is generated that simplifies the payment of tax through online banking (by going to bank's tax payment and filing service and adding the payment type "Revenu Québec download code". To make payment, copy and paste the code and it will be allocated to the correct tax accounts).

What Are the Eligibility Criteria to Use the Quick Method in Quebec?

For GST/HST purposes, annual taxable sales must be less than $400,000. QST requires that annual taxable sales be less than $418,952.

What Are the Rates Used for the Quick Method?

If 40% or more of your sales are from goods that were purchased for resale (e.g., all objects or things that may be perceived by the senses and are movable at the time of supply: a vehicle, animals, furniture, etc.):

- GST Rate = 1.8%
- QST Rate = 3.4%

If your cost of goods sold is less than 40% (effectively, you are a service-based business):

- GST rate is 3.6%
- QST rate is 6.6%

For both GST and QST purposes, you are eligible for a 1% credit on your first $30,000 of sales when using the Quick Method.

To use the Quick Method in Quebec ,you must complete form FP-2074-V, Election Respecting the Quick Method of Accounting.

How Do You Register for a Quebec Payroll Account?

If you operate a business in Quebec, you are required to register both Federally (see above) and in Quebec. Similar to the Federal registration, there are three options for registering a payroll number with Revenu Québec:

- ONLINE: If you already have a Business Number, you should register for a *clicSÉQUR My Account for Business* with Revenu Québec. Once you have completed your registration, log in to *My Account for Business* where you can then apply for a payroll account directly. in the "Source Deductions and Contributions" section.

- PHONE: You can also call Revenu Québec to register for your payroll number.

- MAIL OR FAX: The application for registration, form LM-1-V will need to be filled out for the sections that you are applying which would "deductions at source" in this case. You can also apply for a Business Number at the same time, if you haven't already done so. Note that you will need to enter your Quebec Enterprise Number (NEQ) and your Business Number obtained from the CRA. The LM-1-V allows the business to get a Quebec identification number which is required for all tax files.

How Do You Pay Monthly Remittances (Deductions at Source) to Revenu Québec?

Amounts to be remitted to Revenu Québec include Quebec Pension Plan (QPP), Quebec Parental Insurance Plan (QPIP), Quebec Health Services Fund (QHSF), and Quebec Income Taxes. Quebec employers are also required to pay CNESST and CNT. Note that QPP and QPIP include an employer portion, while QHSF, CNESST, and CNT are all 100% payable by the employer. RQ will also advise you of whether your filing frequency is monthly or quarterly.

Below are remittance and payment options for RQ:

- ONLINE (using Business Banking): Most banks will allow you to set up the Quebec DAS forms and pay online through the business banking service.

- ONLINE (using RQ *clicSÉQUR My Account for Business*): You can submit your DAS by going to your business account with RQ and completing the source deduction form by filling out the appropriate fields. Once complete, RQ will provide you with a "payment code". You can then go to your business banking account, add this payment type, and simply enter the code to make payment.

- MAIL: RQ will also send you a form for monthly deductions at source. This will need to be completed and a cheque enclosed with it for the amount payable. If you don't have the payroll form from RQ, you can create a document which lists the following fields and amounts owing for each:
  - Period to which payroll relates
  - income tax withheld
  - QPP (employee and employer)

- QPIP (employee and employer)
- QHSF (employer only)
- CNESST (employer only)

If paying by cheque, similar to CRA, you should mail it a few days in advance to ensure it is received by the due date and thereby avoid penalties.

Revenu Québec has a comprehensive guide on source deductions and contributions.

> ➢ DAS needs to be paid to both CRA and RQ, separately, when you are an employer in Quebec.

Year End Salary/Dividend Declarations

In addition to the T4 and the T5, which are submitted to CRA for salaries and dividends respectively, Revenue Quebec also requires that you submit RL1s and RL3s. The deadline for submission, which is February 28th, is the same as CRA's.

What You Need to Know about Corporate Taxes in Quebec

In addition to the Federal tax return that is submitted to CRA, corporations resident in Quebec also have to submit a separate corporate tax return to Revenue Quebec. The information required on the corporate tax return is similar to what is required for CRA. Most Canadian corporate tax software has a module for Quebec.

Some of the key differences with respect to corporate taxes are as follows:

- In Quebec, if corporate taxes payable are not paid within two months, then interest will apply on the balance due. This is in contrast to CRA, which allows small business corporations to pay their corporate taxes payable within three months without levying interest.

- The corporate tax number for Quebec corporations ends in IC0001.

- The combined Federal and Provincial corporate tax rate in Quebec is 26.6%, while the small business corporate rate in Quebec ranges between 12.2% and 20.5%, depending on the number of hours worked by employees in the corporation. Essentially, your corporation must have employees that work a total of 5,000 hours per year to be considered a small business in Quebec and be entitled to the small business deduction. The maximum number of hours per employee, per year is 2,000 hours.

- You have the option of submitting your Quebec Annual Return with your corporate tax return. Any changes to your corporate information have to be submitted directly through the Registraire des Entreprises portal.

APPENDIX B: SALES TAX IN OTHER PROVINCES

While many Canadian provinces have harmonized their sales tax with the Federal government by charging HST, there are some provinces that have a distinct sales tax regime.

Below is a table of sales tax rates by province:

Province	Type	GST	HST	PST	Total Rate
Alberta	GST	5%			5%
British Columbia	GST + PST	5%		7%	12%
Manitoba	GST + PST	5%		7%	12%
New Brunswick	HST		15%		15%
Newfoundland & Labrador	HST		15%		15%
Northwest Territories	GST	5%			5%
Nova Scotia	HST		15%		15%
Nunavut	GST	5%			5%
Ontario	HST		13%		13%
Prince Edward Island	HST		15%		15%
Quebec	GST + QST	5%		9.975%	14.975%
Saskatchewan	GST + PST	5%		6%	11%
Yukon	GST	5%			5%

There are 4 provinces in which there is a distinct sales tax rate, that is not part of GST/HST and for which you need to register separately and file returns. These provinces are British Columbia, Manitoba, Saskatchewan, and Quebec (see Appendix 1).

British Columbia Provincial Sales Tax (PST)

The B.C. provincial sales tax (PST) is a retail sales tax that applies when a taxable good or service is purchased, acquired, or brought into B.C. for use in B.C., unless a specific exemption applies.

The B.C. sales tax rate of 7% applies to the following categories:

- The purchase or lease of new and used goods in B.C.
- Goods brought, sent, or delivered into B.C. for use in B.C.
- The purchase of:
  - Software
  - Services to goods such as vehicle maintenance, furniture assembly, computer repair
  - Accommodation
  - Legal services
  - Telecommunication services, including internet services and digital and electronic media content, such as music and movies
  - Gifts of vehicles, boats, and aircraft

There are also a number of exceptions for goods and services on which PST is not required to be collected, including the following:

- Food for human consumption (e.g., basic groceries and prepared food such as restaurant meals)
- Books, newspapers, and magazines
- Children-sized clothing
- Bicycles
- Prescription medications and household medical aids such as cough syrup and pain medications

The chart below shows the reporting periods which is dependent on how much sales tax you collect:

PST collectable per year	Ongoing reporting period
$3,000 or less	Quarterly, semi-annual or annua
More than $3,000 up to $6,000	Quarterly or semi-annual
More than $6,000 up to $12,000	Monthly or quarterly
More than $12,000	Monthly only

For more details relating to B.C. PST, please refer to the guidance on the government of BC website.

Note: As of April 1st, 2021, B.C. started requiring businesses that are not resident in B.C. but sell goods and services on which the PST is applicable to B.C. residents to register for PST. Full details on this can be found here.

Manitoba Provincial Retail Sales Tax (RST)

The Retail Sales Tax (RST) is a tax applied to the retail sale or rental of most goods and certain services in Manitoba. The tax is calculated on the selling price, before the GST (Good and Services Tax) is applied.

The provincial sales tax rate is 7%.

Your business is required to be registered for sales tax if:

- you carry on business in Manitoba, selling taxable goods or services at retail
- you are a manufacturer, wholesaler, or importer in Manitoba (directly or through an agent)
- you bring into or receive in Manitoba, taxable goods for use by your business
- you are an out-of-province business that solicits and sells goods in Manitoba
- you are a mechanical or electrical (M&E) contractor performing work in Manitoba
- you operate a retail business in Manitoba on a temporary, short-term or intermittent basis

You are not required to be registered for Manitoba sales tax if:

- your business sells only non-taxable goods or services
- you are a contractor who only supplies and installs goods into real property, and you buy all goods from sellers registered for Manitoba retail sales tax
- your business's annual taxable sales volume is under $10,000, and you buy all goods from sellers registered for Manitoba retail sales tax

For more details relating to Manitoba PST, please refer to this pamphlet issued by the government of Manitoba.

Saskatchewan Provincial Sales Tax (PST)

The Saskatchewan sales tax applies to taxable goods and services consumed or used in Saskatchewan. It applies to goods and services purchased in the province as well as goods and services imported for consumption or use in Saskatchewan. Both new and used goods are subject to tax.

The Saskatchewan sales tax rate of 6% applies to the following categories:

- accounting and bookkeeping services
- advertising services
- architectural services
- commercial building cleaning services
- computer services
- credit reporting or collection services
- dry cleaning and laundry services
- employment placement services
- engineering services
- extended warranty and maintenance contracts
- legal services
- lodging services
- real estate services
- repair or installation services related to tangible personal property
- security and investigation services
- telecommunication services
- telephone answering services
- veterinary services
- services to real property

Certain goods are exempt from PST in Saskatchewan, including:

- basic groceries
- reading materials
- agricultural equipment
- prescription drugs and medicine

For more details relating to Saskatchewan PST, please refer to this information bulletin issued by the government of Saskatchewan.

ABOUT THE AUTHOR

My name is Ronika Khanna. I am a Chartered Professional Accountant (CPA), Chartered Accountant (CA), and Chartered Financial Analyst (CFA), and the founder of Montreal Financial, an accounting, tax and financial consulting services business. After having worked as an accounting professional for several companies, both in Canada and Bermuda, including with PricewaterhouseCoopers (PwC) and ING Risk Management Limited, I decided to launch my own business, focusing primarily on the accounting, tax, and financial needs of small business owners, start-ups, and independent contractors.

I have helped numerous small businesses with their financial, accounting, and tax reporting over the years, which has allowed them to run their businesses more effectively and profitably.

I would love for us to connect, which you can do by subscribing to my biweekly newsletter, where I discuss topics of interest to small businesses, provide tax and QuickBooks tips, and links to my latest articles. You can also email me at ronika@montrealfinancial.ca.

If you have specific questions about starting your business, accounting or tax, you can also set up a consultation directly by visiting my services page or sending me an email.

If you require assistance with your incorporation or corporate maintenance, please contact my colleague, Brock Hanly, at bhanly@incorp.limited.

OTHER BOOKS BY RONIKA KHANNA

Starting a business from nothing is an intimidating prospect! Launch your enterprise with confidence using this step-by-step guide to starting your Canadian sole proprietorship. Learn about the registration process, setting up your bank accounts, HST & GST, accounting, invoicing, and, of course, how to pay yourself. Starting your own business doesn't mean you have to start it all on your own. Find the answers you need in this handy, easy-to-read book.

For small business owners, administrators, and bookkeepers, this book will help you to understand everything you need to know about paying yourself using small business corporation dividends. Step by step instructions guide you through preparing and submitting your own tax filings to the government, avoiding pitfalls, and ensuring that you can access the money your business has earned.

QUICKSTART
— YOUR —
QUICKBOOKS
A COMPREHENSIVE BEGINNER'S GUIDE TO
WORKING WITH QUICKBOOKS ONLINE

CANADIAN EDITION

RONIKA KHANNA

QuickBooks is the world's most popular accounting software—and a powerful tool for small businesses. But it can be intimidating to learn on your own. Graduate from novice to intermediate user with confidence as you explore over 250 pages of tips, tricks, and detailed procedures for fully integrating QuickBooks Online with your business.

Starting a business or becoming self-employed opens up a whole new world of tax considerations. This book will guide you through the fundamentals to ensure that you pay the taxes you need to but no more than that. In learning about the different types of tax and the sorts of deductions that unincorporated businesses are entitled to you can have a better understanding of your small business tax and save time and money.

SMALL
BUSINESS
TAX FACTS
AN EASY TO UNDERSTAND TAX GUIDE FOR
CANADIAN SMALL BUSINESS OWNERS

RONIKA KHANNA

www.ingramcontent.com/pod-product-compliance
Lightning Source LLC
Chambersburg PA
CBHW071607210326
41597CB00019B/3432